Professional Killers:

An Inside Look

Veteran police writer Burt Rapp is author of *Loompanics Criminal Justice Series*. These other fine books by Burt Rapp are available from Loompanics Unlimited:

- *S.W.A.T. Team Operations*
- *The 211 Book: Armed Robbery Investigation*
- *Shadowing and Surveillance*
- *Undercover Work: A Complete Handbook*
- *Sex Crimes Investigation*
- *The Police Sniper: A Complete Handbook*
- *Vehicle Theft Investigation*
- *The B & E Book: Burglary Techniques and Investigation*
- *Bodyguarding: A Complete Manual*
- *Shoplifting and Employee Theft Investigation*
- *Interrogation: A Complete Manual*
- *Homicide Investigation*
- *Deep Cover: Police Intelligence Operations*
- *Armed Defense: Gunfight Survival for the Householder and Businessman*

Professional Killers:
An Inside Look

Burt Rapp

Loompanics Unlimited
Port Townsend, Washington

PROFESSIONAL KILLERS: An Inside Look

© 1990 by Loompanics Unlimited
Printed in USA

Published by:
Loompanics Unlimited
PO Box 1197
Port Townsend, WA 98368
Loompanics Unlimited is a division of Loompanics Enterprises, Inc.

Photos by Burt Rapp
Illustrations by Kevin Martin

ISBN 1-55950-054-9
Library of Congress
   Catalog Card Number 90-063507

Contents

Introduction

Killers for hire probably have been with us as long as there have been people on Earth. Killing for pay is a trade at least as old as prostitution, but not as widely acknowledged.

Researching this book quickly showed that the subject is vast. There have been many professional killers in history, and probably more than ever are operating today. It would be possible to fill an encyclopedia with information on all types of hired killers and related topics. This is why it's important to draw a few lines, and to narrow the definition.

Today's definition isn't as broad as those of the past. Mercenaries operate as organized bodies, not as individuals, and their purpose is usually to seize power or territory, not kill a specific individual. Mass killers, such as those who place bombs aboard aircraft, are usually terrorists seeking to commit an atrocity, not kill a specific person. State-paid executioners operate within the criminal justice system, enforcing the law, although one segment of opinion considers capital punishment cruel, inhumane, and uncivilized. Vigilantes and lynch mobs kill for idealism, not for pay. Police "death squads," as seen in several South American countries, operate with the protection of the law.

We'll omit various psychopaths and killers for pleasure. The story of Charles Manson and his gang is fascinating, but irrelevant, as they didn't kill for pay. Robert Smith, who committed mass murder in a beauty shop in Mesa, Arizona, in 1966, was a thrill killer, doing it for yuks and not for bucks.

We must also skip over certain ideological killers, such as the killer of Archduke Franz Ferdinand in 1914. Although this incident precipitated World War I, it was not a contract hit.

Today's professional killer operates strictly outside the law. He may work for a private party or a government. As a government agent, he kills the enemies of his country on foreign soil, subject to foreign law. If he's caught he's liable to prosecution, beyond the protection of his government.

Today's contract killers vary from unskilled street thugs to highly skilled and trained professionals, using high-tech tools of assassination. Some contract killings are so neat and professional that the police don't even spot them as murders. Others are bungled jobs, bringing grief to everyone, including those who paid for the assassination.

There really are no rules. Some private contractors are very skilled, lucky, or both. By contrast, there have been some instances of ineptitude among state-hired killers and their employers. We'll see some instances of amazing incompetence by major espionage and intelligence agencies.

Assassination is an art form more than a science. There's room for individual style, because most "jobs" are approachable in several different ways. Reviewing many professional hits shows that most killers executed them in ways that reflected their styles and preferences, as well as operational dictates.

There's a certain amount of confusion about professional killers, their tools, methods, and targets. This is partly because many operate in secret, but also because of propaganda. If political objectives are involved, each side will try to discredit the other. If innocent people are in the cross-fire, it offers an opportunity to label the assassin as a killer of women and children, and his intended target passes into relative obscurity.

An outstanding example of propaganda is the flurry of accusations surrounding hired killers working for and against Israel. In their youth, as leaders of the Irgun and the Stern Gang, Menachem Begin and Itzakh Shamir both used hit men to eliminate inconvenient people, but in their old age they denounce Arabs who use similar methods against Israel. Indeed, before Israel became a state, Zionist assassins killed British officials such as Lord Moyne, British Middle East Minister, and Swedish Count Folke Bernadotte, UN Middle East Mediator. They also planted bombs, such as the one that blew up the King David Hotel in Jerusalem, killing 91 people, including 15 Jews.

Although we'll skim over the history of assassination for the sake of gaining perspective, there isn't room to cover the history of hired killers exhaustively. Likewise, we'll have to pass over many examples of killing for pay in our own time, simply because there are too many incidents, or they're not documented well enough. For example, there's a largely untold story of assassinations during the Vietnamese War, when the C.I.A. launched its Phoenix Program to kill Viet Cong leaders. On the other side, V.C. hit squads killed village head men and other Vietnamese who worked conspicuously for the Saigon Government. There were tens of thousands of such deaths, but because these were clandestine affairs, most were inadequately recorded and today it's almost impossible to reconstruct the story.

This book will describe professional killers, their tools, and most importantly, their methods of operation. Killers for hire have an unusual way of looking at the world, but they seek self-preservation as ardently as do their victims. For this, they try to take as few chances as possible, and adapt their methods to minimize the risks. Only by understanding their tactics is it possible to provide protection and to defeat them.

This book is for the professional police officer, the private security specialist, and the citizen and taxpayer. Although few of the murders which take place in this country are professional "hits," it's important for the investigating officer to recognize one if he encounters it. This will allow him to make a quick investigation and avoid wasting time if the chances of solving it are poor, as they usually are.

It's different for the police officer assigned to protecting a witness. People in various witness protection programs are often gang members who defect and spill their knowledge to prosecutors in return for special consideration. Part of the deal is keeping them alive, both long enough to testify and after their usefulness is over, so that they may enjoy the rewards. Most government witnesses survive, but there have been a few conspicuous failures. The officer on protective detail must understand that his adversary is a skilled professional, and must be aware of the ways in which pros operate.

The private security specialist may have a client worried about assassination. Understanding the mind-set and methods of the professional contract killer will help forestall him, and add to the client's security.

The citizen and taxpayer gets both the worst and the best of the deal. He pays the bill for the typically ineffective police investigation into a professional hit. The cheering aspect is that he's the least likely to become the victim of a high-priced contract specialist.

1

The Professional Killer in Fiction

Fictionalized treatment of the professional killer varies from fair to simply awful. Some writers are serious, and do their research fairly thoroughly, presenting an almost-plausible story. Perhaps the best one is *Day of the Jackal.*

Day of the Jackal

Fredrick Forsyth's book was outstandingly successful, and followed by a motion picture that kept very well to the printed version. The plot line is simple. Dissident French military officers hire a free-lance private killer to assassinate President de Gaulle. The killer, who goes by the code name of "Jackal," makes extensive preparations, first obtaining several passports under false names. For one, he assumes the name of an English boy who died in childhood, obtaining the passport through legitimate channels. He then steals a Danish passport from a Dane who resembles him superficially.

He goes to a custom gunsmith in Belgium to order a special sniper's rifle. This rifle comes apart to fit inside the struts of a crutch. He orders special ammunition, with exploding bullets. The gunsmith makes these by placing a drop of mercury inside the cavities of hollow-point bullets, then sealing the orifices. This is a technical error, as mercury would quickly form an amalgam with the lead, negating the effect.

The killer enters France, and the French police, alerted by the Secret Service, set about finding him before he can kill de Gaulle. The killer changes his identity several times as the police discover each one. His advantage is that he has a source of information inside the French Government, enabling him to keep one step ahead of the cops.

The plan is to shoot de Gaulle while he is at a public ceremony. The French detective in charge of the case notices an open window overlooking the square, and enters the building. A shoot-out takes place, and the "Jackal" dies without killing de Gaulle.

The fault in this story is that a professional assassin would never undertake to kill the leader of a major power. The odds against his escape are simply too great. As recent history proves, it's possible to kill an American president, a Swedish prime minister, and even a German government official, but escape is another matter.

The Mechanic

"Mechanic" is one underworld slang term for a professional killer. This book by Brian Garfield also became a motion picture, starring Charles Bronson. Unlike the inoffensive central character of *Death Wish*, Garfield's mechanic is more flamboyant and takes too many risks. His greatest mistake is "adopting" an apprentice, a young punk with whom he forms an intensely paternalistic attachment. He teaches his young ward all he knows, but instead of being grateful, the apprentice plots to kill his mentor and take over his practice. Bronson dies after downing a poisoned drink, and the punk returns home, thinking that he is now the heir. However, Bronson left behind a car bomb, in case he didn't return, and this blows up the punk in a scene of fitting revenge.

Brass Target

This piece of revisionist historical fiction deals with a plot to kill General George Patton. The book was by Fredrick Nolan, and after some changes in the plot, became a movie, with a star-studded cast. Among the actors were George Kennedy, Robert Vaughn, Bruce Davison, Edward Herrman, John Cassavetes, and Sophia Loren.

A band of corrupt U.S. Army officers carry out a complex plot to steal captured Reichsbank gold after the end of World War II. Robert Vaughn and Edward Herrman, playing two homosexual colonels, are also the two central characters in the plot, and they take drastic steps to ensure that they're not caught. Patton is the commanding general, and he intends to ram-rod the investigation into the theft, wherever it may lead. It therefore becomes necessary to hire a couple of European killers to begin eliminating people who might lead to the ringleaders. Vaughn and Herrman hire a German hit man, who eliminates several army officers whom they see as weak links. It also becomes necessary to eliminate Patton, and for this they send one of their co-conspirators to hire a master craftsman, an elite professional killer. To forestall any possibility of a link to them, they have the other officer eliminated after he makes the connection. John Cassavetes, however, is on the target list. The German killer meets his end when he comes after Cassavetes.

The elite professional killer, known as "Shelley," constructs an elaborate plan, first obtaining a special gun that shoots a rubber plug at a velocity low enough not to break the skin. Disguising himself as an American soldier, the killer enters Patton's motor pool and gimmicks his car door so that the window won't close. He then steals an army truck and parks it in the road around a corner, where he knows that Patton's car will pass. Once Patton's car stops, the killer fires, the plug breaking Patton's neck. Cassavetes arrives too late to save Patton, but he eventually tracks down the killer and dispatches him with his own weapon.

Sword of Gideon

This 1986 film by HBO Productions is based on George Jonas' book, *Vengeance*, and deals with one assassination team that the Israeli Government sent out to exact reprisals after the killing of Israeli athletes in Munich during the 1972 Olympic Games. The film is a simplified and fictionalized version of the book, with the names of most characters changed. The only ones remaining under their own identities are Golda Meir, the Israeli Prime Minister at the time, and various victims, such as Wael Zwaiter, an Arab shot to death in Rome. The sequence of events differs greatly from actuality, and the emphasis is on the humaneness of the Israeli assassins. A totally fabricated scene, for example, has the Israeli team leader in the hospital waiting room with a bouquet of flowers when the wife and daughter of Mahmoud Hamshari learn of his death. The family's grief moves him, and there's a later tearful scene during which he expresses some remorse that his actions had shattered the Arab's family.

Apart from the extensive condensation of events, and the omission of many incidents, the film is a fairly good rendition of the practicalities of assassination. Although the film format doesn't allow showing the mass of detail work and the careful preparations involved in setting up a hit, it presents enough to give the viewer a "feel" for the task.

The Liquidator

This 1966 British film is a satire on the government-sponsored killer. A totally inept man, played by Rod Taylor, attracts the notice of a British intelligence officer by saving his life during World War II. This life-saving encounter is a bungled job, because the liquidator is a poor shot and hits the German attackers only by accident. Years later, British security is rocked by various scandals, and the chief decides that the government can't afford another public trial or defection, for fear that it would undermine public confidence in the government's security. He proposes that, instead, the department hire a liquidator to dispose of any suspected traitors, without trial, and making it look like an accident. The British officer under him remembers Rod Taylor, whom he believes to be a cold-blooded killer with ice water in his veins, and he recruits him back into government work. After extensive training in weapon handling and unarmed combat, Taylor is apparently fit for duty. Actually, he's very squeamish, and doesn't look forward to his first assignment.

This is disposing of a female government employee suspected of treason. The plan is for him to push her under a train on London's underground. He can't do it, and instead seeks out a professional killer, sub-contracting the job to him.

This film is a comedy, but has real-life counterparts. It's not too far-fetched to imagine a government quietly liquidating potential traitors. Likewise, ineffective people in government service are hardly news.

Prizzi's Honor

This Jack Nicholson film deals with killers in the employ of organized crime. Nicholson plays a Mafia killer who marries a female killer for a West Coast mob. Although this film is not exactly a "comedy," we can't take it very seriously as an accurate reflection of mob life or mob hits.

Fiction vs. Reality

Fictional accounts are for entertainment, and novelists can take liberties they would not if they had to go out to kill someone for real. Plots tend to be much more complex than necessary, because the story of a simple murder doesn't make entertaining reading. Likewise, weapons tend to be exotic, even approaching science-fiction in their complexity.

Some plot themes are realistic. That of the government killer slaying people within the country for suspected treason is not too wild, as stories of various South American police "death squads" have come to light.

The real-life professional killer doesn't take unnecessary chances. Furthermore, he's extremely conservative in accepting assignments. As a killer for hire, he wants to live to spend the money he earns, and escape is always important in his planning.

Another sharp difference is that organized crime figures tend to keep their "business" strictly apart from their personal lives. They do not take their work home with them, and certainly don't let their wives know the details of what they do for a living. It's inconceivable that a mob killer would marry another in the same line of work, even if she were an attractive female.

With all that, fiction sometimes approaches real life. The important point for the professional killer is that he does not try to imitate fiction. More than most other people, he must understand the difference between "tube training" and reality.

2

Killing is Easy

The United States has a very high murder rate, compared to most Western countries. Violence is part of our culture, for better or for worse.

A common myth, fostered and perpetuated by popular writers and self-styled "experts," is that killing another human being is a terribly difficult thing to do, leading to massive remorse and psychological after-shocks. This is nonsense. Very few people who commit murder are remorseful afterwards. It's one thing to kill a small child in a traffic accident. It's another to kill someone who appears to deserve it.

We have many laws, and other regulations, regarding killing in various forms. This is because killing is very easy.

Police officers, for example, carry deadly weapons, yet an array of laws and departmental regulations govern when and how they may use deadly force. They live under a legal fiction that they may use deadly force only to "stop" a felon, not to kill him. They're allowed to stop anyone from committing a crime or completing a deadly attack upon another person. They also may use deadly force when attacked by someone with a deadly weapon.

It's hard to see how "stopping" someone with gunfire can oc-cur without inflicting life-threatening injury. Many of those shot by police officers die of their wounds.

American police officers also have an array of non-lethal and "less-lethal" weapons to subdue a suspect without inflicting life-threatening injuries. Chemical sprays, for example, overcome an individual by making his eyes tear, interfering with his respiration, etc. Batons are for various painful but non-lethal blows to the arms and legs. Electronic "stun guns" also incapacitate a violent person by pain and shock, without using a large enough current to be dangerous.

The armed forces also are under various restrictions. In peacetime, there are "rules of engagement" to govern their actions in trouble spots around the globe. During war, a military axiom is that it's better to wound an enemy soldier than to kill him, because an injured soldier requires at least two others to carry him to safety, and other enemy personnel to care for him once he reaches a field dressing station or hospital. Just as in peacetime, though, it's hard to fire bullets and shells at an enemy without risking killing him. "Shooting to wound" is a myth.

Adaptation to taking human life varies with the individual and the methods available. With some, a remote assassination is preferable. A car bomb is more impersonal than shooting a target while close enough to see his face.[1]

Another viewpoint is that moral restraints are fallacies, invented by politicians and religious leaders as tools to manipulate people into serving them. There's good reason for accepting this viewpoint, because it's so blatantly true in many cases.[2]

Whatever the professional killer's moral outlook, he has adapted it to the needs of his job. He may kill for God and Country, or simply for bucks, but his conscience doesn't bother him.

Sources

1. *Vengeance,* George Jonas, New York, Bantam Books, 1984, pp. 221-222.
2. *Killer Elite,* Bradley J. Steiner, Boulder, CO, Paladin Press, 1985, pp. 75-83.

3

History

Hired killers have probably been part of the human race since before recorded history. However, even after the start of written history, hired killers did not get the recognition they deserved. There always appeared to be something shameful about hiring someone to do the dirty work, even if the employer were the emperor, as in the case of Nero.

Rome

Nero had a mistress, for whom he cared more than he did for his wife, Octavia. His officials, acting under orders in 63 A.D., framed Octavia with accusations of adultery, to facilitate a divorce. Octavia was, even in exile, an inconvenience, and Nero ordered her to commit suicide. When she balked, he had his government goons slit her arteries, and place her in a hot bath to speed up the hemorrhage.[1]

At times, it seemed that assassination was the Roman way of political succession, but not all ambitious Roman politicians were willing to get their own hands smeared with blood. Domitian, an emperor who had made his reputation through many executions, fell victim to a plot in 96 A.D. An assassin, posing as a messenger, stabbed Domitian in the groin. This was a bad beginning, and led to a free-for-all, with Domitian grappling with the hired killer. The killer's strength won in the end, and he inflicted enough wounds on Domitian to kill him.[2]

The Arabs

The term "assassin" originated with the Arabs, who used selected killers who reinforced their devotion with the drug hashish, a drug made from marijuana. The original cult of "hashishins" was started by a petty potentate named Aloadin, who lived in Persia. He also inspired his killers by promising them paradise if they died in the cause. Paradise was a garden with beautiful girls, for presumably endless sex.[3] The leader, originally known as "Hasan i Sabbah," used his professional killers as an instrument of political power. There is no list of all of the people they assassinated, typically dispatching them with edged weapons. They were so effective, however, that the term "assassin" is still with us today, having survived a few translations and crossed the ocean.

The Renaissance

The tradition of political assassination continued with the Roman Catholic Church of the Renaissance. The Italy of that era had a corps of professional killers, known as "condottiere," to do the dirty work for those who did not want to dip their fingers in blood. One of the earliest documented assassinations, the killing of Giuliano Medici, had the support of Pope Sixtus IV.[4]

The Mafia

The Italian "MAFIA," an acronym for "Morte Alla Francia Italia Anela" (Death to France is Italy's cry), was originally an underground movement against French occupiers. With Garibaldi's unification of Italy in 1860, the Mafia turned toward organized crime. In Italy, the Mafia became a sort of underground government, and existed because of various degrees of toleration by the legitimate government.[5] In America, though, the Mafia flourished, and became the prototype of the kind of criminal gang that furnished Hollywood with raw material for its films.

Two Mafia hit men killed a man named Labousse in New Orleans in 1881, in reprisal for informing on the local Mafia boss, Esposito.[6] This was perhaps the first Mafia killing in America, and it was the precursor of many. It hasn't been possible to keep track of all such hits in our country, as they've been too numerous. Some were very bold. Mafia hit men shot to death David Hennessey, New Orleans' police commissioner, on the night of October 15, 1890, in front of his home.

Another police officer who lost his life in a gang hit was Joseph Petrosino, a New York City Police Department investigator who went to Italy to search in Italian police files for information on "Mafiosi" who had immigrated to America. The New York branch of Italian organized crime went under the name of "Black Hand." In Palermo, Sicily, Petrosino walked into an ambush one night, having been lured there by a man who claimed to have information he wanted. Shooters opened up on him, filling his body with over 100 bullets.[7] Petrosino's career and fatal encounter with the Black Hand was the basis for a 1940s motion picture of that title.

Italians did not have a monopoly on killing for hire. In 1874, a New York gang calling itself the "Whyos" set up shop doing free-lance enforcement. At the time, Irish gangsters dominated the New York scene. Whereas Mafia enforcers had worked to carry out the wishes of their gang bosses, the Whyos did killings and beatings for anyone who had the price. Their rate for a killing was $100.[8]

Italian gangsters, however, soon fell into the habits of their Roman ancestors and used assassination as a means of determining succession to power. One of the first big transfers of power was the demise of Chicago's "Big Jim" Colosimo. A hit man named Frankie Yale put a bullet through his head on May 11, 1920, clearing the way for the younger, more ambitious Johnny Torrio.[9] Colosimo had imported Torrio from New York to help his Chicago operation, and Torrio decided to go it alone. Torrio soon found that he had to use enforcers himself to retain his empire. A minor gangster named Joe Howard went into business hijacking some of Torrio's alcohol delivery trucks. Torrio felt he had to do something. Alphonse Capone, a roly-poly New York hood of Neapolitan extraction, served as trigger-man for Torrio. On May 8, 1924, Capone shot Joe Howard to death in a saloon on South Wabash Avenue.[10]

Gangs in Chicago were not exclusively Italian, several being Irish, or Irish-dominated. Dion O'Bannion, leader of a rival gang, performed several unkind acts to alienate Johnny Torrio, and on November 8, 1924, three of Torrio's enforcers walked into O'Bannion's flower shop on North State Street. Frankie Yale, their leader, was acquainted with O'Bannion, and shook hands with him. He held on to O'Bannion's hand, presumably to keep him from escaping, while his two partners shot him to death.[11]

Murder, Inc.

The corps of professional killers was evolving. The "Saint Valentine's Day Massacre," which took place in a garage in Chicago on St. Valentine's Day in 1929, was a pre-emptive strike against a mob led by George "Bugs" Moran, one of Capone's rivals. Moran was not on the premises when the killers, imported torpedoes from New York, arrived. Dressed in police uniforms, they lined the seven occupants of the garage up against a wall and shot them to death with a submachine gun and a shotgun.

Events now moved quickly, and a New York gang leader named Charles "Lucky" Luciano saw the need for a change of leadership to facilitate new ways of management. A carefully co-ordinated liquidation of over 30 "Mustache Petes," as old-style gangsters were derisively called, took place on September 11, 1931. This is the event which was fictionalized and dramatized in the Hollywood film, *The Godfather,* a few years ago. The basic concept of a corps of highly mobile enforcers, moving around the country to cope with local problems, was born.

The official title of the evolving organization of professional hit men was "Murder, Incorporated." It became officially sanctioned at a national crime syndicate (also known as the "Combination") meeting in Kansas City in 1934. "Murder, Inc." actually consisted of several murder squads, not all of which were ever uncovered and prosecuted. Their training and professionalism were uneven, as they were a para-military force born in combat and constantly evolving. Several trends quickly became prominent.

One was the recruitment of experienced thugs, drawn from various vicious gangs in the toughest parts of the country. East

New York/Brownsville was one such locale. Another was the equal opportunity policy followed. Ethnic barriers were fading, as Murder, Inc. took in Jewish and other gangsters to fill its ranks. Yet another trend was abandonment of the submachine gun in favor of lower-profile weapons, such as the icepick.[12] This quiet weapon accounted for about one-third of their hits during the evolving years.

Lepke Buchalter, a New York Jew, was probably Murder, Inc.'s most intellectual and talented boss. He got the credit for devising the modern jargon, such as "contract," "hit," etc., and he devised a business and compensation plan that even today serves as the basis for paying hired killers. Prices in those days varied from $1,000 to $6,000, depending on the nature of the target and the risks involved. An expense account and personal-injury fund covered contingencies. Buchalter developed the system of importing "talent" from other cities for hits. This provided killers with no obvious connections to their targets, but it also provided a tactical advantage. The unfamiliar faces would not alarm the targets as locally-conscripted hit men would. Another point was that there was minimal chance of conflict of loyalties, as there might have been if a local boy was used to assassinate a target. A local might have gone to school with his intended target, or be married to a relative, etc.

The total body count is uncertain. One estimate is 9,000 for the country.[13] Murder, Inc. was able to operate in almost total secrecy for six years, until the bottom fell out by a defection. One of the Brooklyn branch's hit men was a shabby, short gangster of Jewish extraction named Abe "Kid Twist" Reles. The nickname was for his habit of twisting arms. An old murder charge, dating from 1933, led to his arrest on February 2, 1940. To save his neck, Reles offered the Brooklyn, New York,

District Attorney, William O'Dwyer, inside information on Murder, Inc.[14]

Reles disclosed what he knew, which was limited only to the Brooklyn outfit. Compartmentalization and observing the "need to know" principle maintained security for the rest of the national operation. Still, Reles' information was sensational enough. He told O'Dwyer about 85 murders his group had committed. He named Buchalter as the boss, and Buchalter, in self-defense, put out contracts on Reles and other possible informers. O'Dwyer arranged for a police guard for Reles and several other witnesses.

At about 6:45 A.M. on the morning of November 12, 1941, Abe Reles went out of the window of a sixth-floor bedroom at the Half Moon Hotel, in Coney Island, Brooklyn. Five New York City police officers had been on guard when this happened, and their accounts do not agree with those of independent witnesses, such as the hotel's assistant manager and another office worker whose window overlooked the setback where Reles' body had landed. The official version was that Reles had constructed a makeshift rope from some bedsheets and wire, and had tried to escape from custody. The rope had broken under his weight, and Reles had fallen to his death, dying from a fractured spine. The five police officers found themselves charged with neglect of duty, but no criminal charges.[15]

The Murder, Inc. revelations led to some prosecutions. Two hit men, Harry Strauss and "Bugsy" Goldstein, were electrocuted on June 12, 1940. Two more, "Happy" Maione and "Dasher" Abbandando, went to the electric chair on February 19, 1942. Buchalter followed, in March, 1944. However, Murder, Inc. was dead only in the eyes of the media. It was still functioning. Albert Anastasia, who had been one of Murder, Inc.'s ace triggermen, had risen to greater things and gotten involved in a power struggle. His rivals got a contract out for him, and Anastasia met death in a barber's chair on October 27, 1957. Anastasia was seated in the chair in the barbershop at Manhattan's Park Sheraton Hotel, when two assassins, led by "Crazy Joe" Gallo, a Brooklyn thug, entered and opened fire. Operationally, it was a sloppy job. Only five of the ten bullets fired struck his body. Anastasia, however, was in no position to criticize the marksmanship, for he died on the spot.[16]

Gallo survived Anastasia for fifteen years. He was intent on pursuing his career as a mob figure, and became involved in a spat with the Columbo faction. On April 7, 1972, Gallo, his wife, and a few friends went nightclubbing for his 43rd birthday. During the early morning hours of April 8th, they sat down to a meal at Umberto's Clam House on Mulberry Street in New York's Little Italy. Several men walked in and shot him. Accounts of the shooting vary. One states that four killers did the job.[17] Another claims that there were only three hit men, and that Gallo died with the first shot.[18] There are other discrepancies, but the final result was never in doubt: Gallo died that night.

Some Recent Hits

American hit men continue to do well. One more recent victim was Joseph Yablonski, a rival of "Tough Tony" Boyle for the presidency of the United Mine Workers Union. Boyle recruited three hoods to shoot Yablonski to death, but when they invaded his home, they found his wife and daughter there, too, and liquidated them as well.[19] Charles Bronson starred in a motion picture portraying Yablonski's killing.

One of the murkiest contract killings was the shooting of Martin Luther King, Jr., in Memphis, Tennessee. There have been several books about King's life, and at least one to explain partly the people and circumstances involved in his murder, but none reveals the entire story in a satisfactory way.[20]

One fact is sure: the history of contract killings will continue. It's a convenient way of putting inconvenient people out of the way.

Sources

1. *A Criminal History of Mankind,* Colin Wilson, New York, G.P. Putnam's Sons, 1984, p. 209.

2. *Ibid.,* pp. 223-224.

3. *Ibid.,* pp. 281-282.

4. *Ibid.,* pp. 340-346.

5. *Ibid.,* pp. 540-542.

6. *Ibid.,* p. 542.

7. *Ibid.,* p. 547. This is probably a sensationalized account of the events. Virgil Peterson's version, on Page 461 of his book, *The Mob,* states that two men fired a total of four shots at Petrosino, and that only three bullets hit. One shot hit him in the brain, killing him instantly.

8. *Murder, USA,* John Godwin, New York, Ballantine Books, 1978, p. 49.

9. *A Criminal History of Mankind,* p. 551.

10. *Ibid.,* pp. 551-552.

11. *Ibid.,* p. 552.

12. *Murder, USA,* p. 140.

13. *Ibid.,* p. 141.
14. *The Mob,* Virgil W. Peterson, Ottawa, IL, Green Hill Publishers, Inc., p. 227.
15. *Ibid.,* pp. 231-232.
16. *Murder, USA,* pp. 144-145.
17. *Ibid.,* p. 149.
18. *A Criminal History of Mankind,* p. 569.
19. *Murder, USA,* pp. 158-159.
20. *The Murkin Conspiracy,* Philip H. Melanson, New York, Praeger, 1989.

4

Today's
Hired Killers

There's a vast difference between the professional killer and the amateur, even though the amateur may be spectacularly successful in carrying out the killing. The professional plans carefully, because killing's only half the job, survival being the other half. Let's look at one outstanding amateur killing to see the differences:

On November 24, 1963, Jack Ruby shot Lee Harvey Oswald, the alleged assassin of President Kennedy, in the torso at point-blank range with a "snubby" .38 Special revolver. The site was the basement of Dallas police headquarters, where officers were preparing to transfer Oswald. The bullet hit Oswald in the spleen, liver, and right kidney, puncturing a major blood vessel on the way. This injury proved fatal within an hour and 40 minutes, despite emergency room care. Officers present, who knew Ruby, arrested him on the spot.

Jack Ruby, despite his reputation as being connected with organized crime, was not a professional killer. He did not plan his act well, instead acting on impulse and opportunity. A "pro" would not shoot his target with a handgun in a police station. He would also have his escape planned so that he'd survive to spend his fee.

Today's contract killers vary widely in abilities and experience. Government-trained professionals are probably among the highest grade killers in existence. Government officials in charge of deciding expedient terminations have their departments of dirty tricks, and need only official clearance.[1]

The private person seeking to hire a contract killer has to be very wary regarding who he hires, unless he's a member of an organization that has professional killers on the payroll or on retainer. Organized crime has its own network, and channels for assigning contracts.

One Case:
How *Not* To Do It

A professional "hit" occurred on December 23, 1987, in Phoenix, Arizona. James Gregory Haley, described in testimony as "inept," accepted a contract to collect a $15,000 drug debt for his employer, Eric Zarska, of Philadelphia. The person who owed the money was Richard Graybill, who lived on the west side of Phoenix. Haley arrived in Phoenix without a change of clothing, and had difficulty finding the address at first. He bolstered his courage with a large dose of cocaine. When he knocked on the door of the house, Graybill answered, and a scuffle ensued. Haley shot Graybill to death, then went through the house eliminating potential witnesses. In a bedroom, he shot to death Graybill's 20-year old daughter, Shelley, and her friend, Beau Collier, aged 15.[2]

After the shooting, Haley, who was covered with blood, took a taxi to the airport, where he placed a collect call to his employer to request that he wire him money for air fare home. He also took the murder weapon back with him, instead of ditching it in a remote place. These actions left a conspicuous trail which the Phoenix police had no trouble following.

Incredibly, this case wasn't unique. Another "professional hit man" took a taxi to the place where he did the shooting, and the taxi driver remembered him.[3]

Today's Pros

There are several types of professional killers. At the lowest end of the scale are the immature, adventurous personality types who read the mercenary magazines and dream of heroic deeds. These are the Walter Mittys and "Wannabe" types. The wannabes are macho men, with weapons in their fists, and earning big money for their martial prowess. Wannabes are in the same class as those who attend store-front karate schools and hire themselves out as bodyguards. Anyone who employs such a type is betting his freedom, and perhaps his life, on the slim chance that this type has the skill and the emotional stamina for the job.

Another type of flaky killer is the low-grade thug who works cheaply. He may botch the job, and will certainly point a finger if captured. This type is as much a liability to his employer as he is an asset.

Probably the worst type is the drug addict, who accepts any paying job so that he may continue to support his habit. His need is so desperate that he'll agree to anything for money, even if it's beyond his skill. The other side of the coin is that, if captured, police can make him confess by withholding his drugs. The person who hires a doper can expect disappointment, because dopers are simply unreliable.

Likewise for alcoholics. While alcohol is not an illegal substance right now, addiction to it produces personality changes that are intolerable in a professional. In many ways, alcoholics are as flaky and unreliable as dopers. Placing any trust in one, for a matter, literally, of life and death, is foolish.

The top-of-the-line is the ex-military or ex-law enforcement professional who decides to go into private practice. Such a professional already has had training and time to develop his skills. He also has the personal contacts that can be valuable in running his business. Such people are rarely in the headlines because they're very good at their jobs. Amateurs and bunglers get caught. The competent professional does not, except for cases of very bad luck.

Training and Background

Both police and military receive training both in weapons use and in unarmed combat. There are certain significant differences between the two. The police officer's more likely to practice unarmed combat and use of the baton on an almost daily basis, if he's assigned to a fairly busy locale. Police training focuses on non-lethal use of various weapons, and using only the force necessary to complete an arrest. The police officer is unlikely to have to shoot anyone during his career, and his weapon skills will usually take in only the police handgun. Members of special armed response teams take much more weapons training.

The military man will have training in the use of a greater variety of weapons, as well as knives used in silent killing techniques. He'll also have the opportunity to take training in explosives and demolition, especially if he's in one of the elite units. Some training won't have any application in civilian "jobs," as assassins rarely use tanks and artillery in their work. However, military training focuses on killing.

The law or military officer also has access to certain commodities during his active years, and if he's thinking about private practice later, he'll plan and prepare in advance. Police officers, for example, routinely confiscate weapons and drugs from suspects. Although there are occasional scandals when a supply of drugs vanishes from a property room, obtaining contraband is much easier when there is no arrest or prosecution.

The police officer who pats down a suspect and finds drugs or a concealed weapon may decide not to make any arrest. If he simply confiscates the goods, the suspect will be grateful to have avoided arrest and prosecution, and certainly will not lodge a complaint to get his property back. This is how police officers obtain guns and knives to use as "throw-down" weapons, and drugs used to pay off informers. This sort of informal confiscation provides a way for the future pro for hire to obtain untraceable weapons and materials for his work.

Police work also allows access to other items. When investigating a burglary at a doctor's office, for example, the officer can slip a syringe and a few needles into his pocket. He can also take a vial or two of drugs which can be useful later. The paralyzing drug, "Anectine," for example, is not what a doper would take in a burglary, but if the responding officer picks it up, the doctor may never miss it, or may think that he ran out and forgot to restock it.

The military man has access to other types of materials, such as plastic explosives and demolition devices. It's easy to purloin small arms ammunition and explosives. During any training course, small amounts can disappear. On operations, large quantities of supplies are "unaccounted for." If the future pro is in the supply services, he can fudge paperwork to make off with actual weapons. For example, he can strip down several damaged handguns, rifles, or submachine guns, destined for the scrap pile, and put together a functioning weapon from the parts.

Membership in a police or military organization allows "networking," informal contacts between old comrades and people with similar interests. This can lead to contacts for assignments after retirement.

Finding and Hiring the Pro

Personal and professional contacts are the key to finding and hiring a professional killer. Unlike in fiction, the person who needs a killing done doesn't ask a cab driver, nor does he hang around bars waiting for a thug to appear.

There are, of course, "barroom commandos" who gather for a few drinks and spout macho talk. Taking any of these seriously is a major error. The most obvious reason is that anyone who really has engaged in contract killings does not brag about it in bars, where an informer may be listening. Another is that the client who hires such a person, even if the job goes as scheduled, can expect the details of his contract to be the subject of discussion during another drinking session.

Probably the worst way is to answer classified ads in a macho magazine. In one notorious case in 1986, *Soldier of Fortune* ran a "Gun For Hire" ad placed by two men who later were accused of murdering on a contract. One client who contacted the two men asked them to kill his wife for him, making it look like a robbery. According to Palm Beach, Florida, County Sheriff Richard Wille, the husband allegedly paid $20,000 for the contract.[4] Criminal prosecutions resulted, and *Soldier of Fortune* Magazine was on the receiving end of a civil suit for that incident.

The reason that personal and professional contacts are the key to bringing client and contractor together is that there must be a bond of mutual trust, based on long acquaintance and reputation. Professional contracts such as these are not topics to discuss with strangers, unless they come well recommended.

The first qualification for the private citizen who wants to hire a pro is to have enough money to pay well. One source states that $30,000 is a typical price.[5] The killers who placed the ads in *Soldier of Fortune* allegedly charged $20,000, and they performed badly enough to get caught. It appears that $30 thousand is rock-bottom for a competent job, and expenses are extra.

The money involved precludes the ordinary "working stiff" from hiring a class act professional. More likely, the organized crime or "legitimate" business executive will be the one seeking such services. If the executive has a close friend in law enforcement, he may ask him for advice. This involves a serious risk, if the friend turns out to be a "straight arrow." Another route is to ask the corporation's security director, who is usually a retired police officer. Again, this requires that the security director be basically sympathetic to the needs of his employers, and have ethics flexible enough to allow him to make the contact.

The reason for starting with a cop or ex-cop is that these people are familiar with underworld figures, and some may know people who accept heavy contracts. A security executive employed by a multi-national corporation is almost certain to have such contacts, because company officials may need a troublesome labor leader eliminated, or may decide that termination is the best way to deal with a difficult foreign politician. Not all police or former police types know whom to contact. The "beat cop" will surely know a few local thugs, but nobody with the skill to do a first-class job. An officer with experience in an organized-crime detail probably knows who does these jobs with class and skill.

Small-town police chiefs and politicians are unlikely to know any professional killers. Their experience is usually limited to barroom commandos.

Membership in certain veterans' organizations can also lead to contacts. This doesn't mean the typical veterans' group with members who get together each night for a session of boozing and telling war stories. Specialized groups, such as those limited to members of elite outfits, are the ones more likely to have a few of these very special contractors among the membership.

Another, and very limited, possibility, is the veteran of a special military organization who runs a shooting or self-defense school, and who maintains many contacts with his former buddies. The shooting school operator may not want to undertake a contract himself, but he may be able to refer a client to someone who kills for hire.[6]

Protocol

There's a certain procedure to follow in engaging a killer for hire. The accepted courtesy is that neither party states outright, at the first meeting, that he wants someone killed, or that he will kill for pay. The form is always a third-party discussion, or even a hypothetical one. This is to avoid admitting guilt when each side isn't sure of the other. A practical point is that the other party might be "wearing a wire," or recorder. The discussion might begin this way:

"Where would someone who needs a certain person put out of the way make contact with a person who could do the job?"

"I don't know off-hand, but I'll ask around and see what I can find out."

Phrased this way, the discussion isn't incriminating to either party. No jury would convict on the basis of these words, even with a tape recording as evidence.

Another meeting might occur, after each party has made a few inquiries about the other, and satisfied himself that this is not an entrapment scheme. At this meeting, it may be possible to fix the terms, and negotiate a price.

Price depends upon several factors. One is what the client can afford to pay. Another is what the contractor wants for the job. This, in turn, depends upon the difficulty anticipated. A high-profile job, involving the liquidation of a public or semi-public figure, can run into hundreds of thousands of dollars, partly because of the risk, and partly because of the contractor's not being able to work again if his identity comes to light.

In organized crime, there is a scale of payment, usually lower than in private industry. The organization pays for the job, and guarantees legal defense in case of discovery. The employee benefit plan goes a step further, guaranteeing subsistence for the contractor's family. One point we've noted about organized crime killings is that often they involve "torpedoes" from out of town. These imported killers are not known locally, and their appearance won't alarm the target, who might run for cover if he saw any local hirelings approaching him.

Payment usually consists of half the fee in advance, with expenses "up front."[7] Expenses can be moderate or heavy, depending on the circumstances. If the pro has to travel far, procure an exotic and expensive weapon, and stay at an expensive hotel, his cash outlay can run into thousands. The client, on his part, has the right to demand that the pro keep expenses down to a reasonable amount. The true pro will not object to this. Anyone who accepts an assignment with the intent to indulge in high living by looting the expense account is not a true professional, and will quickly acquire a reputation as a flake.

Payment is always in cash. Pros don't accept Master Charge or checks. There's a certain honor system here, in that the pro trusts the employer to pay the balance after he completes the job. It's a poor idea to try to defraud a professional killer. While it's true that the pro cannot go to the police if his employer cheats him, he has another recourse that makes it unwise to withhold payment from him.

Discretion

Keeping a low profile and remaining discreet are the hall-marks of the true professional. He's acutely aware that protecting the interests of his clients and former clients is vital to his livelihood, as well as his survival. He does not drop names carelessly, or brag about former assignments.

Today's professional has learned from the errors of the past. He (or she) is highly skilled, and well paid for putting his talents at the service of people who value death as highly as life.

Sources

1. *Killer Elite,* Bradley J. Steiner, Boulder, CO, Paladin Press, 1985, p. 5.
2. *Arizona Republic,* August 25, 1989.
3. *Hit Man,* Rex Feral, Boulder, CO, Paladin Press, 1983, p. 106.

4. Scripps Howard News Service, April 6, 1986.
5. *Hit Man,* p. 91.
6. One of the author's personal contacts ran such a school for several years. A former military man, he was fascinated by weapons and violence, and kept himself well-informed on resources for hire.
7. *Hit Man,* p. 92.

5

Government Killers

Governments have had hired killers throughout recorded history, but Twentieth Century operations are the ones which interest us. We'll begin with Soviet operations, for convenience. It's easier to find information about Soviet assassins because Western governments publicize Soviet assassination incidents, while keeping a discreet silence about their own efforts in this area.

The Soviet Secret Police has been known by various sets of initials during its short history. "GPU," "OGPU," "NKVD," "MVD," and others preceded the current designation: "KGB." The Soviet Army Intelligence Service, concerned with military espionage, but often overlapping, has always been the "GRU." Both services, concerned with maintaining discipline in the ranks, employ professional assassins to keep the troops in line. Under the Stalin regime, the main point seemed to be to show anyone thinking of disloyalty that Stalin's secret police had a very long arm, reaching even across the ocean, to liquidate a defector or traitor.

During the summer of 1937, a Captain Maximov died mysteriously, falling from the observation deck of the Eiffel Tower, in Paris.[1] This was one of the first recorded instances of someone whom the Soviet Regime wished dead coming to an end under murky circumstances.

Stalin Purge Liquidations

The Stalin Purges of the 1930s resulted in a great many deaths, and some of the targets included agents of the Soviet espionage apparatus stationed abroad. When the secret police wished to liquidate an agent stationed on foreign soil, there was a simple way of getting their hands on him; recall. The agent would receive a message that he was needed back at headquarters in Moscow for "consultations" or even a promotion. He'd leave for Moscow, and never return. This trick got old very quickly, and some didn't heed their recalls. One such was Ignatz Reiss, who deserted the Soviet Secret Service on July 17, 1937. The home office mobilized its resources to find him, and got results. After going to ground in Switzerland, Reiss had gotten in touch with an old friend, a German woman named Gertrude Schildbach, who was a fellow Soviet agent living in Italy. She betrayed him to the secret police to save herself from suspicion, and on the night of September 4, 1937, a two-man hit team accosted Reiss outside a restaurant in Switzerland, dragged him into a car, and put seven bullets in his body and five more in his head.[2]

Walter Krivitsky

The case of Walter Krivitsky got great notoriety in America, because it took place in Washington, D.C. It was tied in with the Reiss killing, because the two men had been friends. Both were Jews originating from Southern Poland, and they'd shared duty stations before the purge hit Reiss. Krivitsky was alarmed, and decided to defect. He and his wife arrived in New York in December, 1938, where he started making contacts among his Jewish friends, trying to earn his way in the new world.

American intelligence and security agencies didn't seem to be interested in him, for a very good reason. He'd been a Soviet agent in Europe, not America.

He started trying to earn a living in this country by selling magazine articles on his life and experiences, and this may have attracted attention. On March 7, 1939, while having lunch near Times Square with the editor of a Jewish publication, Krivitsky saw three men take a table nearby. He recognized one as Sergei Basoff, also a member of the Soviet Secret Service. Basoff wanted to speak with him, just a "chat," but Krivitsky was understandably suspicious, and did not go off alone with him.

Krivitsky continued to try to sell himself to the American government, and did get an audience with a minor State Department official who was interested in Soviet affairs. He also had a hearing before the House Un-American Activities Committee. None of this came to much, as far as American intelligence agencies taking any benefit from it, but it alarmed the Soviets enough to inspire them to take drastic action. Among the pieces of information Krivitsky kept in his head was the infiltration of the British establishment by Soviet recruits, an affair which exploded after the war. Krivitsky did reveal to British officials enough information for them to uncover a certain John Herbert King, a government employee who had been passing information to the Soviets.[3]

Krivitsky even traveled to London during 1939-1940, to undergo a debriefing by MI-5, the British Security Service. As the British security organizations were already infiltrated with Soviet agents, the people at Moscow headquarters cannot have failed to note the efforts Krivitsky was making to hurt them. He came back to the United States, and in February, 1941, was living at Washington's Bellevue Hotel. A maid found him dead in his room, a bullet in his head and a pistol in his hand, on

February 10th. It was a mystery for anyone who suspected murder. There were even three suicide notes, which a forensic expert stated were in Krivitsky's handwriting. Opinions of Krivitsky's associates at the time were that the Soviet assassination apparatus had produced forged suicide notes, and had planted them when they had killed him. Obtaining a key to the room was not a difficult problem, nor was faking the suicide. An important reason for suspecting murder, though, was Krivitsky's warning his associates that, if ever they heard that he had killed himself, not to believe it.[4]

Leon Trotsky

The year before, on August 20, 1940, Leon Trotsky had allowed a relative stranger into his study in Mexico. This man, a deep cover Soviet agent operating under the name of "Jackson," killed Trotsky with an ice axe the moment he was alone with him.

Trotsky had been Stalin's main rival during the power struggle of the 1920s, after Lenin's death, and had gone into exile after losing to Stalin. Trotsky continued to lead a movement against Stalin, a fact that has become submerged under the torrent of anti-Soviet propaganda published in the West. Trotsky was a continual thorn in Stalin's side, and one of the contributing causes of the purges of the 1930s in Russia. For Stalin, getting rid of Trotsky became a high-priority project.

This wasn't easy, for Trotsky was well-guarded, living in a villa in Mexico. His staff of bodyguards accompanied him wherever he went. The way the Soviet assassination bureau chose was to insinuate a killer into his confidence. The killer's background is murky, and it's almost impossible to separate fact from carefully built-up cover story. "Jackson" also passed himself off as a Spaniard, using the name "Ramon Mercader del

Rio," fabricated for him by the Soviet Secret Service. The basic facts are that Jackson got in to see Trotsky because he had some introductions from people Trotsky trusted. Jackson may have also gained Trotsky's confidence because they were both originally Jewish, or at least Jackson claimed to be so. Jackson brought the murder weapon with him, under his jacket, and killed Trotsky in a particularly messy way. Trotsky did not die immediately, and Jackson did not die at the hands of Trotsky's bodyguards. The Mexican government, after having a psychiatrist examine Jackson, tried and convicted him of murder. Jackson served 28 years in prison, never admitting his Soviet connection, before the government paroled him. Upon his release, he boarded a flight to Prague, and that was the last anyone in the West heard of him.

The Birth of SMERSH

World War II saw routine executions of traitors and suspected informers in the various guerrilla wars which flourished at the time. The NKVD set up a special counter-espionage and assassination bureau, first known as "SMERSH," a contraction of "smiert spiona," which means "death to spies." Later, the name changed, formally or informally, to the "Department of Wet Affairs." This translates from the Russian idiom roughly as the "Department of Dirty Work." Under various names the department has continued functioning to this day.

Jan Masaryk

The post-war period saw political assassination used in its purest sense, as a raw tool of political power. One killing which made headlines on both sides of the Iron Curtain was the "suicide" of Jan Masaryk, then Czechoslovak Foreign Minister, on March 10, 1948.[5] Masaryk, a Czech politician who was apparently not enamored of the communist system, supposedly killed himself by jumping from a window in the Czernin Palace. However, there's good reason to believe that he was "defenestrated" by Soviet agents.[6]

The Gas Gun Assassinations

A widely-publicized case from the cold war period was that of Bogdan Stashinsky, a KGB killer who liquidated two Ukrainian freedom movement leaders in West Germany. Stashinsky began his career as a Soviet informer masquerading as an East German, living and working in East Germany, keeping an eye on Russia's former enemy. In 1958, he got a change of assignment, probably because he was skilled at passing as a German. Soviet officers issued him a special assassination weapon, a single-shot poison gun, which he was to use on his targets.

There have been contradictory accounts of the exact nature of this weapon. Some published material refers to it as a "cyanide gun." Another account is unspecific as to the exact chemical used, but describes the weapon fairly well.[7]

This was an aluminum cylinder, slightly over six inches long by ¾ of an inch in diameter. Inside, a firing mechanism would shoot out a small amount of liquid, as a spray or mist, for an effective range of about 18 inches. Whether the device worked on compressed air, spring action, or a small primer charge is unclear, but it made little noise. The mode of use was to get close to the target and spray the liquid into his face. A second choice was to spray into the chest area, because the fumes were lighter than air and would rise to engulf his nose and mouth. Allegedly, it took only one inhalation to be fatal. The poison was supposed to act instantly, but because it takes time for blood to circulate, it actually took a couple of minutes for the victim to die.

Spraying poison fumes into the air was dangerous for the assassin, who risked getting caught in the spray if any wind blew it back at him. To cope with this problem, the Soviet armorer issued Stashinsky antidote tablets, to take before he used the weapon, and a breakable ampule of inhalant to counter the effects if he got caught in the spray. One account stated that the tablets were potassium thiosulfate, an antidote to cyanide poisoning. Another stated that, because the unnamed poison worked by constricting the arteries leading to the brain, the tablets and inhalant were vasodilators.

In October, 1958, Stashinsky went to Munich, assuming the identity of a real West German citizen. He stalked Lev Rebet, his first target, until he decided upon a place for the attempt. This was a staircase at Rebet's office, where Stashinsky arranged to be walking down as Rebet was ascending. Stashinsky carried the weapon inside a rolled-up newspaper, and when he got close to Rebet, pointed it at his face and triggered it. Continuing to walk downstairs, Stashinsky heard Rebet stumble, but he didn't look back. He walked to a nearby canal and dropped the weapon into the water, as it was designed as a one-shot throw-away. Rebet had lived just long enough to climb a couple of flights, where he died from what appeared to be a "heart attack."

Stashinsky's next target was Stepan Bandera, who also lived in Munich. For this assignment, the Soviet armorer issued him a new double-barreled version of the assassination weapon. Stashinsky made several trips to Munich, stalking his prey, and finally succeeded in October, 1959. Stashinsky was in the lobby of Bandera's apartment house when Bandera unlocked the outer door on his way in. Bandera was carrying a bag of groceries as he struggled with the door lock. Stashinsky accosted him in the doorway and stopped him with a question, asking if the lock worked. Bandera turned his face to Stashinsky, who let him have both barrels. Like Rebet, Bandera lived long enough to climb a couple of flights of stairs before collapsing, but he did not die until in the ambulance, several minutes later. The autopsy report stated that he'd died of cyanide poisoning.[8] Stashinsky dropped his weapon into a canal, and went back to Soviet controlled territory.

The Bulgarian Incidents

Georgi Markov was a Bulgarian defector who worked for the overseas broadcast service of the British Broadcasting Corporation. His strange death in 1978 seemed almost certainly to have had a connection with the Bulgarian Secret Service because of his activities, and he had stated that he feared assassination or kidnaping. One afternoon, while standing in a bus line in London, he felt a jab in the back of his right thigh. He turned around and saw a man, who appeared to be a foreigner, leaving the scene holding an umbrella. That night, he developed a fever, and three days later, died in a hospital. An autopsy showed that a tiny ball of platinum/iridium alloy was embedded in his flesh under the skin. The ball had four tiny holes drilled in it to hold the poison. The nature of the poison remained unknown for the moment.[9]

Vladimir Kostov was another Bulgarian defector, living in Paris. One day in August, 1978, he felt a sharp pain in his thigh while riding on the Paris subway. He developed a serious fever, but recovered after several days. After hearing of what had happened to Markov, Kostov had himself checked out, and doctors found a similar metal ball embedded in his thigh. Upon removal, this turned out to be identical to the one found in Markov's body. Further analysis showed that the chemical agent was probably ricin, a very toxic alkaloid derived from the castor bean.[10]

Kostov was never sure whether anyone had stabbed him with an umbrella, as he didn't notice anyone who might have been responsible for injecting the pellet into him. In both this and the Markov case, the assassin was never identified.

There was widespread belief that the Bulgarians were behind the shooting of the Pope, although the connection never became clear. An Italian investigation into the affair produced inconclusive evidence. What is obvious is that Mohammed Ali Agca fired at the Pope during one of the Pope's public appearances. Agca used a 9mm Browning P-35 pistol, putting the Pontiff into the hospital but not killing him.

American Efforts

The Central Intelligence Agency has always had a covert operations division, under various names. During the early years, it was known as the "Plans Division." One function of the clandestine services was to be ready to carry out an assassination, known by the euphemistic term, "Executive action."

Tangible preparations began early. U. S. Patent #3,060,165, filed July 3, 1952, deals with the preparation of toxic ricin, listing the names of five people as co-inventors. The interesting part is that this patent is assigned to the "United States of America, as represented by the Secretary of the Army."

When James V. Forrestal, Secretary of Defense, went out of a window in the psychiatric ward of Bethesda Naval Hospital in 1949, there were suspicions about the manner of his death. Although the official verdict was "suicide," it seemed incredible that a depressed psychiatric patient could open a supposedly secured window in a psychiatric ward. A right-wing view was that Forrestal had been liquidated by "liberals" because he was an impediment to them. No evidence surfaced, however, to indicate that this defenestration had been other than suicide.

One of the best-known American efforts to kill a foreign head of state was the plot against Patrice Lumumba, President of the newly-founded Congo Republic. During 1960 and 1961, elements in the CIA feared that Lumumba was too anti-American for their tastes, and they looked into the prospects of getting rid of him by various means. One method explored was to use poison, suggested by a CIA doctor, Sidney Gottlieb. Another was to take him out with a sniper.[11] Neither method proved practical, for various reasons, and Lumumba came to an end in 1961 at the hands of a rival political group in the Congo. There's very good reason to conclude that Lumumba's rivals benefited from American aid and financial support.[12]

The United States Government also worked on several plans to kill or discredit Fidel Castro. Once President Eisenhower broke diplomatic relations with Cuba, elements in the CIA began exploring ways to incapacitate Castro. In December, 1959, the CIA's Colonel J. C. King, in charge of western hemisphere operations, suggested in a memo to Allen Dulles that Castro's elimination was desirable.[13]

CIA technicians explored several approaches. One was to lace Havana's TV studios with LSD, so that Castro would ingest the drug and become incoherent during his next address to the nation. Another was to drug his cigars. Yet another was to somehow dose Castro with thallium salts, to make his beard fall out.[14]

More serious plots were in the works. A CIA executive, Robert Maheu, reached an accord with John Rosselli, a high boss in the American Mafia, to have Castro assassinated. The fee was reportedly $150,000, but the plot failed to get off the ground. Another attempt proposed was to poison Castro with botulism toxin, but this, too, failed for unknown reasons.[15]

Although the attempt to make Castro's beard fall out was patently absurd, it had a precedent in the World War II efforts of the OSS. One idea worked out by Stanley Lovell, a research scientist working for the OSS, was to make Hitler's mustache fall off. There were other attempts to inject poisons into Hitler's food. None succeeded.[16]

Mind Control

A main avenue of experimentation by the Central Intelligence Agency during its early years was using psychological techniques to produce a dehumanized killer under perfect control.[17]

A person who would allow himself to be transformed into a mindless assassination tool was the agency's dream, because there always have been problems with sending assassins off on missions. They may get cold feet, and they may tell who sent them if caught. Providing a suicide pill to someone on a secret mission doesn't always work, as the U-2 incident of 1960 proved. Francis Powers, the captured pilot, not only did not take his poisoned needle, but talked freely to Soviet interrogators, even though he was not tortured.

Morse Allen, a CIA official during the early days, was able to run several successful experiments with young secretaries in his office. He hypnotized some, giving them post-hypnotic suggestions to steal secret papers. When the secretaries followed these instructions, he got bolder. He hypnotized another, giving her the post-hypnotic command to shoot someone upon a cue.

The girl did not know that the pistol was empty, and she pulled the trigger. Still, such experiments under controlled conditions did not prove that the technique would work in the field.

There were several approaches to the problem of creating a programmed assassin, or "Manchurian Candidate," after Richard Condon's novel of that name. In the fictional version, communist brainwashers kidnap and program an American soldier to live a normal life until activated by a code phrase; "play a little solitaire." He then would be ready to accept orders relating to his mission.

In real life there were several hurdles to cross. One was motivating the individual to undertake a very dangerous mission, which could well cost him his life. Another was to induce him or her to kill in cold blood. Yet another was not to incriminate his masters. This could come about by inducing amnesia regarding the hypnosis, and the entire sequence of events that followed his recruitment as a secret agent. Another was to induce him to forget the assassination as soon as it was over. Yet another was to program him to commit suicide as soon as he had completed his mission, to avoid capture and the possibility of being cracked open by other psychological techniques.

Another possible technique was to induce hypnosis upon an unwilling subject, and program him to do the killing. This was most interesting, because if it were possible to gain access to someone close to the intended target, the effects could be catastrophic for the targeted country. To have a foreign head of state killed by his secretary or finance minister would cause disruption far beyond the simple killing. The problem with this proposal was that there was no reliable technique for hypnotizing an unwilling person, and no reliable way to make certain that such a subject would carry out his orders.

Yet another approach was to give a subject hypnotic orders that would enable him to resist interrogation if caught. This, too, worked under test conditions, but nobody felt confident enough to use it in the field.

Inducing amnesia was certainly possible, and indeed had been done to both willing and unwilling test subjects, using both drugs and electroshock.[18] Psychiatrists had long known that application of electroshock therapy would blank out recent or distant memory, or both, depending upon the individual and the amount of shock treatments applied. The agency commissioned a study, done in Canada, to determine exactly how much memory loss was possible using a combination of drug-induced long sleep and a series of industrial-strength shock treatments applied several times a day.[19] Insofar as amnesia went, the experiments were successful. The patients' shocked brains were adequately scrambled. Operationally, the entire affair was a failure, because there was no practical way of applying shock treatments to one's agent once he fell into the hands of the other side's secret police.

As far as is publicly known, the CIA did not succeed in producing a programmed assassin. There's always a possibility of such a program having succeeded under deep cover, because the CIA has managed to create some totally secret and independent subsidiary organizations.

Deep Cover

The CIA has tremendous power and influence. This amounts to more than the public knows, and more than members of Congress know. The CIA has placed its agents in many branches of the government, under cover, to carry out its assignments.[20]

Some personnel are "sheep-dipped," a process of producing phony records and papers to maintain their cover.[21] This process works both ways. It allows the CIA to borrow or recruit men from the armed services for clandestine operations, and it allows the agency to keep some of the covert operators completely divorced from the CIA, insofar as it's possible to trace the paperwork.

The covert operations go deeper than that. Theoretically, a critical aspect of any government department's operations is funding. Only Congress can, ultimately, allocate funds. Some agencies and high executives in the government have "contingency" or non-accountable funds, but these are limited. In any case, they originate in the same office, and may ultimately be traceable. However, the CIA operates certain independent businesses, such as Air America.[22] These are legitimate companies, listed in Dun and Bradstreet and operating in public. They're staffed by a mixture of people, the highest posts going to CIA executives, and other jobs to people who may or may not know that they're working for a CIA-sponsored business.

These CIA-started companies have two purposes. One is to provide resources, obtained from other than U.S. Government sources, for covert operations. The other purpose is to earn untraceable funds. These companies operate at a profit, unlike many government departments, and the profit provides seed money for establishing yet other companies totally removed from U.S. Government gaze or control. This allows CIA agents to operate certain very clandestine activities under very deep cover.

An operation such as this provides the ideal setting for recruiting, equipping, and training a corps of assassins. This would be completely beyond the knowledge or control of anyone in the government except the CIA executive in charge. Let's pursue a hypothetical case, to see exactly how it can be done.

A bank account, containing several million dollars, exists for funding the assassination bureau. The money has come, suitably "laundered," from other CIA business profits. This serves as capital for setting up a new company; "Arizona Associated Enterprises," a name that reveals absolutely nothing about the company's business. Company executives, all sheep-dipped, rent an office in Phoenix, and begin looking for a remote plot of land for special purposes. The Phoenix office serves for purchasing, and as legal headquarters for the company. Company checking accounts are started in nearby banks, with separate accounts for material procurement, payroll, and other functions. The "president" of the company keeps several thousand dollars in cash in an office safe, and more at home, to take care of special needs. Company credit cards provide for normal, above-board business expenses, such as travel and telephone calls.

A scout for the company finds a 500-acre plot in a remote area. The nearest town is 30 miles away, and the land consists mostly of hills. Only one dirt road leads to the site. This makes it ideal for screening out curious passersby, if any. Some construction begins. Specially-cleared workers from another CIA dummy company build storage sheds, living accommodations, and several special-purpose buildings, all sealed and air-conditioned. None of them know who really owns the site or what purpose the buildings will serve. When the job is complete, they leave their tools and surplus materials behind.

With the basic plant in place, the real work begins. Company officers recruit scientists to work on biological toxins. Others build a firing range for training assassins. A gymnasium for physical training and unarmed combat instruction is also part of the plan. Yet other "employees" set up an armory, obtaining materials and weapons with a Federal Firearms License legally obtained from the BATF under company cover. A machine shop begins turning out prototype weapons, such as an umbrella that shoots poison darts, or a cigarette lighter to spray poison gas. Using fiberglass and epoxy, they cast special daggers that don't set off alarms at airport security gates.

Company officers travel to other cities, states, and countries, to produce "cover" organizations for the agents. This involves opening an "office," which is typically a mail drop and answering service, as a foundation. This basic preparation allows starting a business bank account, to support a checking account and company credit card. In today's economy, a credit card can be vital. Most car rental companies, for example, will not rent a car for cash. They require a credit card as a "line" to the renter in case of damage or theft. A company credit card also has the advantage of being instantly transferable, unlike those issued to individuals. Any agent can use the card, under any alias he chooses, for purchases and rentals. "Backstopping" is limited to covering the amounts of transactions, and for this a simple line of credit is enough. During operations, nobody will check further than to assure that the cards are valid and that they will collect their money. If a disaster occurs, leading to the agent's capture, investigators will find only a blind account.

A network of such "companies" makes it possible to prepare an agent with a source of funding and documentation that cannot lead back to the agency or government which employs him. This allows perfect compartmentalization and insulation from the parent government. In some cases, the assassin may not even know he's working for any government. This happens when a case officer recruits an agent from among criminals.

Israeli Hit Teams

After Arab terrorists killed several Israeli athletes during the Munich Olympic Games of 1972, the Israeli Government reacted in its usual fashion and decided to retaliate. Israeli clandestine services sent out at least two assassination teams to kill Arabs on a special list. The list was composed of Arabs suspected of having been involved in the Munich killings, as well as other incidents.

Teams were to operate independently, receiving funds and orders through various indirect ways, and to avoid all contact with Israeli officials. The Union de Banques Suisses, in Geneva, was the focal point for one team's replenishment of funds and operational directives. There was a bank account, serviced by other agents who never knew what purpose the money served, and a safe deposit box in which couriers would leave envelopes for the team and the team could use for feedback.[23]

The basic contingency fund would remain at $250,000, to cover any operational costs that might arise. There were weapons to buy, informers to pay, and sundry expenses, such as travel, accommodations, and meals, to cover. The team kept part of its funds in cash, in the safe deposit box, for quick access and to avoid leaving a paper trail.

The team using the Geneva bank had five members: the leader, an explosives expert, a document forger, a driver, and a "sweeper," whose job it was to linger after a hit and try to dispose of incriminating evidence.[24] They also had a hit list of eleven Arabs.

Their first assassination was in Rome, on October 16, 1972. The target was Wael Zwaiter, a poet and alleged terrorist leader. By means of local help, the team located Zwaiter's address and put him under surveillance. Zwaiter lived alone, and had no bodyguards, which seems unusual for someone reputed to be a noted terrorist leader. The team's leader and explosives expert went into the lobby of Zwaiter's apartment house to wait. When Zwaiter arrived, they identified him and shot him to death with their .22 pistols, pumping fourteen bullets into him.[25] They found out later that Zwaiter was Yasser Arafat's cousin.

The network that helped the Israeli hit team was unofficial, but it exists in every place where there are Jews. Israel claims moral authority over Jews everywhere, and evidence of this is found in the sums of money raised for Jewish bond drives and other causes to benefit Israel in most Jewish communities in the world. Israeli commandos received help from Argentine Jews in Buenos Aires, for example, when they engineered the Eichmann kidnapping in 1960. There is a small but significant Jewish minority in Rome, and some of these probably helped the Israeli team. There may also have been some local thugs involved, giving aid purely for pay. In fact, Jonas' book, *Vengeance,* states that a gang under the leadership of a man named "Tony" conducted surveillance on Zwaiter and provided cars for the job.[26]

The next target on this team's agenda was Mahmoud Hamshari, who was high in the leadership of the Palestinian cause. He lived in an apartment in Paris, and the team planned to take him out with a bomb in his telephone. The plan was to insert the explosive charge into his phone on December 7th, while the apartment was unoccupied, and to kill Hamshari on the morning of December 8th, after his wife and daughter had left for school. The moment came, and Hamshari was alone in the apartment. One agent called him on the telephone from a nearby pay phone, and when Hamshari answered, he gave a hand signal to the explosives expert, who pressed the button on his radio transmitter. Hamshari did not die immediately in the blast, but survived to linger in a hospital ward until he died of his injuries on January 9, 1973.[27]

Another alleged terrorist leader named Abad Al-Chir was the next to go. The hit team found him in a hotel in Nicosia, Cyprus, and their bomb technician placed a bomb under his mattress. A pressure switch armed the bomb, and turned on the radio receiver. A remote radio signal triggered the bomb, but only if there was someone on the bed to arm the bomb. Late in the evening of January 24, 1973, Al-Chir went to bed, and the waiting Israeli agents triggered the bomb. Al-Chir died instantly.[28]

A shooting on a public street was next for this hit team. They shot down Basil Al-Kubaisi on the Rue de l'Arcade in Paris, on the evening of April 6, 1974.[29]

Not all went smoothly for the Israeli hit teams, of which there were at least two operating, each without knowledge of any others. One group, on the track of an alleged Arab terrorist, found him in the Norwegian town of Lillehammer. They shot him to death in front of his wife on the town's main street, discovering afterwards that they'd killed the wrong man, a waiter.[30]

The Future of Government-Sponsored Killings

Assassination is often an expedient way of removing someone from the scene, and in some situations is preferable to more public methods. A wanted criminal, for example, may be the subject of extradition proceedings if he takes refuge in another country, but if no extradition treaty exists between the country that wants him and the host country, there's no way to get him except by clandestine means. Kidnapping can work, but killing is quicker and easier. If the person is wanted for a political crime, chances of extradition under any circumstances are poor.

A clandestine killer, on the other hand, moves silently and quickly. Under the right circumstances, he can solve a difficult problem. The problem may not be a criminal fugitive, but an inconvenient foreign politician or other noted figure. Getting rid of him by clandestine means is cheaper than by military invasion, and enables the instigating government to maintain a low profile in the affair. Denying a lone killer is easier than denying an invasion fleet.

At this writing, October, 1989, President Bush's administration is struggling with what to do about sanctioning assassinations by the CIA. It's clear that the Central Intelligence Agency has, in the past, had a secret mandate to kill certain people, but for the first time, there is public debate on what the government's policy should be. The conflict, for the administration, is publicity versus practicality. It's clear that, whatever the final pronouncement from the White House will be, there will still be that final option, to use in limited and intractable cases.

Sources

1. *The Storm Petrels,* Gordon Brook-Shepherd, New York, Ballantine Books, 1977, p. 69.
2. *Ibid.,* pp. 140-141.
3. *Ibid.,* pp. 156-162.
4. *Ibid.,* pp. 169-177.
5. *KGB/CIA: Intelligence and Counter-Intelligence Operations,* Celina Bledowska and Jonathan Bloch, New York, Exeter Books, 1987, p. 17.
6. Defenestration, or throwing unwanted people out of windows, was a favorite tactic of Soviet assassins, according to a Czech "freedom fighter" who told this account to the author after he fled Czechoslovakia to live in the United States.

7. *Cry Spy!,* Edited by Burke Wilkinson, Englewood Cliffs, NJ, Bradbury Press, 1969, pp. 231-232.
8. *Ibid.,* p. 236.
9. *KGB/CIA: Intelligence and Counter-Intelligence Operations,* pp. 161-162.
10. *Ibid.,* p. 163.
11. *Ibid.,* pp. 84-85.
12. *Ibid.,* p. 86.
13. *Ibid.,* p. 60.
14. *Ibid.,* pp. 60-61.
15. *Ibid.,* p. 64.
16. *The Search for the Manchurian Candidate,* John Marks, New York, Dell Publishing, 1979, pp. 16-17.
17. *Ibid.,* pp. 194-205.
18. *Ibid.,* p. 44, 142.
19. *Ibid.,* pp. 139-146.
20. *The Secret Team,* L. Fletcher Prouty, New York, Ballantine Books, 1973, pp. 289-290, and 313.
21. *Ibid.,* pp. 191-192.
22. *Ibid.,* p. 194.
23. *Vengeance,* George Jonas, New York, Bantam Books, 1984, pp. 85-87.
24. *Ibid.,* pp. 93-95.
25. *Ibid.,* pp. 111-112. Also see *By Way of Deception,* Victor Ostrovsky, New York, St. Martin's Press, 1990. This book, which the Israeli government tried to suppress, describes the network of Jews throughout the world, which the Israeli clandestine services exploit for both espionage and assassinations. It also describes the present-day Israeli killer

teams, known as "kidon," or bayonet. Three 12-man teams take assignments abroad, working in total secrecy.

26. *Ibid.,* pp. 132-138. In this, we have to consider the source. George Jonas was not part of the operation, being a professional writer who published his book after hearing the story from an Israeli who stated that he had been the team leader. Jonas had to go with what the Israeli chose to tell him. In this situation, it's understandable that the Israeli source may well have left out a few details, to protect Italian Jews who had helped him and his men.

27. *Ibid.,* pp. 159-163.

28. *Ibid.,* pp. 166-174.

29. *Ibid.,* pp. 180-190.

30. *Ibid.,* pp. 239-240.

6

Tools and Techniques

Tools and techniques for killing vary with the culture. Although the people who make the decisions like to think that they are totally rational, cultural values affect the choice. In Moslem countries, for example, execution is supposed to be an object lesson, and the killer will often mutilate the body. A common method, used by Moslems in Libya against the Italians and in Algeria against the French, is to cut off the penis and scrotum and stuff them into the corpse's mouth.

Operational requirements also influence the choice of weapons. While totally silent killing is very difficult, there are ways of inducing death less noisy than others. A pistol with a "silencer" is an obvious choice, but not commonly used because the hardware is bulky, illegal in many countries, and would attract attention during customs inspections. A disguised weapon is often advantageous. A weapon obtainable on the local market eliminates the need for importing one. An easily concealed weapon allows the assassin to approach without necessarily alarming the victim.

Assassination or "Accident"

This is a basic decision the hired killer's employer must make. For both political and operational reasons, one may be preferable over the other. At times, circumstances dictate that the assassin make it appear very strongly to be one or the other.

An example is a criminal murder to get rid of a business rival or partner. An obvious murder brings a police investigation, which can cause endless embarrassment and inconvenience to the killer's employer. Another example is a political assassination in a country with which it's important to keep good relations. The killing of Markov in Britain was an example. While it eventually became clear that his death was by design, British police never found a suspect, and almost didn't find the cause of death. This makes it impossible to accuse any foreign government, although the Bulgarians are high on the list of possibilities.

In some cases, death by firearm can appear to be an accident. This absolutely requires several conditions. First, the firearm must belong to the target, and must remain at the scene. This precludes using any weapon which has a paper trail leading to anyone else, even a false identity. Another condition is location. People usually clean their firearms at home, not while driving or at the workplace. Finally, the situation must be credible. If the bullet wound is in the back of the head, death by accident won't wash. A cleaning kit must be nearby to explain the circumstances of the death.

In other cases, there's no point in going too far to conceal the nature of the action. If Fidel Castro had died from a sniper's bullet, for example, there would have been little doubt regarding who ultimately employed the sniper. The only need is to avoid leaving a trail of hard evidence that can point to the sniper's employer.

Weapons

There's a greater variety of hand weapons suitable for assassinations than for military use. Firearms, knives, poisons, and other agents of death have all served well in various situations. Moreover, explosives and incendiaries also have their places.

Choice of weapon depends on several factors. The most important one is the range at which the killing takes place. If it's easy to gain access to the target, contact weapons, such as knives and clubs, are suitable. Beyond this, a firearm is essential. A handgun will do for ranges between six and fifty feet, although some expert marksmen can score hits at longer distances. Beyond fifty feet, a rifle is necessary. If the target is well-protected, a stealth weapon, such as poison, may be helpful.

A second important factor is "target hardening," or the level of protection enjoyed by the target. A target surrounded by bodyguards offers more of a challenge than one who isn't. It's both harder to get to him and to escape afterwards.

The employer's ruthlessness also counts. A lay-off bomb, detonated by remote control, enables destroying the target without being close to the scene, and helps escape. However, any explosive device endangers uninvolved persons, and this is an important factor. Normally, police won't search very hard for the killer of an underworld leader, but if several children die in the blast, there will be an intensive man-hunt.

Another factor is availability. While "gun control" laws don't work well because a criminal can usually obtain firearms on the black market in the most tightly controlled societies, the exact model needed may not be easily available. Explosives are also under tight control in most countries. Commercial-grade dynamite may be obtainable in the black market, but if the task needs a military compound, such as "plastique," the only way of obtaining it would be to steal it from a government armory. This is often hard to do.

Firearms

Firearms are quick and decisive, if the professional is skilled in their use. In certain cases, it may be possible to disguise the act, making it appear accidental, or a suicide.

If the choice is a firearm, a major factor in the decision will be the distance between the assassin and the target. If it's impossible to approach to within a few yards, a sniper's rifle is the obvious choice. Execution by rifle fire, however, is unequivocal. It's impossible to make it look like a suicide or accident, as nobody shoots himself while cleaning a rifle at a range of fifty yards.

Rifles

Caliber is not as important as it might seem. The reason is that operational range will be limited by the need for certainty. It's true that a super-magnum can have an effective range of a thousand yards or more, but this doesn't translate into operational usefulness. Let's examine this closely, to understand the reasons:

The main requirement is to hit the target in a vulnerable area with the first shot. At least two factors can affect this. One is target movement. It takes about $1/10$ of a second for a 30-caliber boat-tail rifle bullet to travel 100 yards if it leaves the weapon at 2500 feet per second. To reach 500 yards takes about ¾ of a second. It will take even longer to reach a target farther out. Using a .458 Magnum flat-nosed soft-point bullet, and a muzzle velocity of 2500 fps, it takes almost a full second to reach 500 yards.

The effect of wind is even more impressive. Our 30-caliber bullet will deflect only $8/10$ of an inch at 100 yards in a 10 mph wind. At 500 yards, the same mild 10 mph wind will blow it over 43 inches to the side, and at 1000 yards, almost 116 inches.

The professional assassin seeks a sure one-shot kill. It's not enough to surmise that the target may succumb to blood poisoning three days later. The killer wants to destroy an organ without which the human body absolutely cannot live. The vital areas on a human target are small. The brain, for example, is about 4 inches wide, maximum, seen from the front or rear, and about 5 inches long, seen from the side. With a rifle-velocity bullet, a hit anywhere in the brain case is fatal, destroying the brain by hydraulic shock. The heart is somewhat smaller than the brain, and its location in the chest is imprecise.

A "kill" may also result from puncturing a major blood vessel, even though the bullet misses all vital organs. This prospect is uncertain, and a professional won't stake his mission on it. While it's true that a "center of mass" shot in the chest is likely to hit the heart, a lung, or pierce a major vessel, this isn't a sure kill, even if rib fragments damage other organs.

Noted assassinations by rifle fire have been at surprisingly short ranges. The first 160-grain bullet to hit President Kennedy, fired from a 6.5mm Mannlicher-Carcano rifle at about 2165 feet per second, struck at a range of 63 yards, and a remaining velocity of less than 1800 fps. The bullet that blew out his brain in a large pink cloud traveled 88 yards. This was not an outstanding feat of marksmanship, especially with the four-power riflescope on top of the carbine.[1]

In 1968, James Earl Ray shot Martin Luther King, Jr. in the throat with a scope-sighted Remington Gamemaster 30.06 rifle.

Ray fired from a room about 70 yards away, as King stood on his hotel room's balcony.[2] That single shot was fatal. This isn't surprising, because the 150-grain 30-caliber bullet still retains over 2600 feet per second of velocity at 100 yards.

In 1979, Federal Judge John Wood, Jr., was shot in the back by a sniper using a .243 caliber rifle. Although the wound was not instantly fatal, within an hour Judge Wood was dead.

Handguns

At this point, it's important to clarify a concept, and relate it to the killer's task. The handgun is less powerful than the rifle, because it's a design compromise favoring compactness, light weight, and concealability. Bullet lethality depends heavily on the site of the hit, and less on caliber and velocity. A small-caliber bullet in the heart or brain produces a much more dangerous wound than a magnum in the hand. Lethality does not necessarily tie in with "stopping power," although a bullet wound which "stops" an opponent immediately is also likely to be life-threatening. This is because a wound which is severe enough to cause the subject to fall down on the spot, and become incapacitated, is one which must produce a severe effect on the body's systems. A handgun can be very effective at close range.

With all that, the instant "stop" is mostly myth. Very few people fall down immediately when shot, whatever the caliber. Even a wound in a vital organ may not produce instant in-capacitation. A bullet which destroys the heart still leaves the victim with a few seconds of consciousness before his brain shuts down from lack of oxygen. This is what has come to be called "the dead man's five seconds," during which he may retaliate against his attacker.

On the other hand, a bullet wound may be eventually lethal, without immediately incapacitating the victim. One which ruptures a blood vessel can kill by loss of blood, without immediately incapacitating or even severely impeding the target's ability to fight back or to flee. Without medical attention, death from infection can ensue days after the shooting. The professional, however, cannot rely on this, as his target may obtain medical care quickly if he survives the attack.

This is why, when the handgun serves as an offensive weapon, it can be smaller and less powerful than one used for defense. When the shooter is not under attack, there's less urgency, and less need to incapacitate the target instantly. A smaller caliber handgun is easier to conceal until needed, and makes less noise.

Figure 1

The .22 caliber automatic pistol is gaining
in popularity with professional killers.

One type of handgun which has come into use by professional killers is the .22 caliber auto pistol. Such a handgun is small, light, and flatter than a revolver, making less of a bulge when carried concealed.

The shirt-pocket sized Sterling Model 302 (shown in Figure 1), although no longer made, is a convenient assassination weapon for two reasons; small size, and easy availability on the second-hand market. Muzzle velocity is less than 1000 feet per second, but this is more than enough to be lethal.

Figure 2

The long-barreled .22 automatic pistol is not
as easy to conceal as the shorter model.

The long-barreled .22 pistol (shown in Figure 2) provides higher velocity and ten rounds in the magazine. With a six-inch barrel, this Hi-Standard pistol is not very concealable. However, it's available second-hand.

The smallest of these have a magazine capacity of six cartridges, more than enough for a killing. Larger ones carry as many as ten rounds, providing a generous margin of safety for contingencies. Both .22 Short and .22 Long Rifle bullets come out of a small, 2″ barrel auto pistol at between 800 and 900 feet per second. This is enough to penetrate the ribs and the skull, assuring a kill if the assassin is a competent marksman.

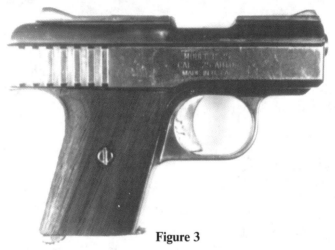

Figure 3

*The Raven P-25 automatic is inexpensive
and widely available second-hand.*

The Raven P-25 (shown in Figure 3) fires the .25ACP cartridge at subsonic speed. Its main advantages are low price and easy availability second-hand, as over 1,000,000 of these have been made.

The .25ACP cartridge develops slightly more kinetic energy than the .22 caliber cartridges because of its heavier, 50-grain bullet, when firing from 2″ barrels. Like the .22, it is lethal at short ranges.

The smallest pistols are the easiest to conceal, but choosing a handgun with a slightly longer barrel has advantages, and doesn't pose a serious concealment problem. A 4″ barrel delivers higher velocities, and is less noisy. A CCI Stinger cartridge sends its 32-grain bullet at over 1200 fps from a 4″ barrel. This develops more velocity and kinetic energy than any .25ACP fired from the shorter barrel. The propellant powder burns inside the chamber and barrel, not in the outside air, and this results in less flash and blast because more of the energy propels the bullet.

American hit men are gravitating towards the .22 caliber pistol, shooting their victims from close range and concentrating on vital areas. Shooting in the back of the head is the hallmark of an "execution" style killing. Some professional killers will first tie the victim's hands, and shoot them while they're sitting or kneeling. Firing several shots into the brain case, spine, and torso makes death certain.

Beretta auto pistols in .22 caliber have seen use by Israeli assassins. Their doctrine is to use a reduced powder charge, which decreases noise, and to fire in bursts of two shots.[3] Israeli hit men compensate for the very low power of their rounds by firing several two-shot bursts into the target's body. They mostly operate in two-man trigger teams, with a third to drive the get-away car.

However, reducing the powder charge also reduces recoil impulse, and this may not be enough to operate the slide, resulting in "short-stroking." The fired case may not eject, and the slide doesn't go back far enough to pick up a fresh round from the magazine. Correcting this will require replacing the pistol's recoil spring with a lighter one to insure correct cycling.

Silencers

The romantic view of the professional killer portrays him with a silencer mounted on the end of his revolver barrel. The reality is quite different. While a silencer has its place, its usefulness is very limited, and the risks involved suggest that there are very few situations in which it's worth using.

First, a silencer, which is really a sound suppressor, works like the muffler on a gasoline engine. It doesn't silence the weapon totally, but just modifies the sound signature so that it's less obtrusive. In plain language, a suppressor doesn't work very well. There are several reasons for this. One is that the suppressor can only trap and slow down the propellant gas, not the bullet, and the sound of a shot actually comes from three sources. The first is propellant gas, which produces muzzle blast. In an auto pistol, the gas leaves the barrel, and a silencer attached to the end will trap it. In a revolver, some gas escapes through the barrel-cylinder gap, and a silencer attached to the barrel can't stop it.

The second is the sound the bullet makes while flying through the air. A bullet traveling at supersonic speed (more than about 1100 feet per second) produces a sonic "crack" which is impossible to suppress. Most rifles fire their bullets at much more than this speed, and this makes a rifle especially difficult to suppress. There is special, "heavy bullet," subsonic ammunition for rifles, designed for use with silencers, but such ammunition sacrifices power and range for this advantage.

Finally, there's the sound of the weapon's mechanism. No silencer will muffle the snap of a hammer or firing pin, or the "clack" of the slide on an auto pistol.

Truth, in this case, is not as impressive as fiction. The silencer has severe technical limitations which greatly reduce its usefulness. One writer of a text on contract killers, who professes to be a former hit man himself, states that a silencer is standard equipment, but he's mistaken.[4] He also describes a silencer designed for use with a .22 carbine, but if this weapon uses supersonic ammunition, part of the effect will be lost. There are also several operational problems with a silencer that limit its use.

First, silencers are strictly controlled by federal law. This means that there is no state in the union where it's legal to own or use a suppressor unless it's registered with the BATF. The second point is its intended use. In many locales, it's illegal to carry a concealed weapon, or even to own one. Problems with the law can develop through bad luck. A handgun can drop out of luggage, the waistband, or fall to the pavement while unpacking a car.[5] It may also be discovered in luggage checked in at an airline counter, even if it's baggage hold luggage. The operator who is "carrying" can explain that he carries a handgun for protection, and this will wash, even with the New York City or Washington, DC, police departments. In some locales, carrying a concealed weapon is legal. In others, it's a misdemeanor. Finally, in some places, such as New York, it's a felony. Still, police officers won't make too much of it if they find a citizen simply carrying a concealed handgun. A prosecution will follow, but the pro can post bail and, if he's traveling under a false identity, disappear before trial.

There is no way to explain a silencer, which will bring a much more thorough investigation. A silencer spells "hit man" to even the most naive rookie. Anyone arrested with a silencer in his possession will face investigation from both local and federal officers.

Another operational limitation is that any situation which is so sensitive that the sound of the shot must be muffled is probably too dangerous for the pro to attempt. If other people are near, they may be able to identify the pro later. In urban settings, the problem is usually to carry out the contract unseen, rather than unheard. There are often enough street noises to cover the sounds of the shots.

If it's absolutely necessary to muffle a shot, a blanket or pillow works very well for small and medium-caliber handguns. Wrapping a blanket around the weapon will reduce the report to a dull "plunk." The problem with this method is that it can jam the weapon, impeding a fast second shot.

Another way to muffle a shot is to let the target's body absorb the full force of the propellant gas. As with suppressors, this works best with an auto pistol. Pressing the muzzle into the target's body requires getting very close, but it both muffles the shot and allows the hot gas to enter the body and increase the destructive effect.

Ammunition

Although there's no substitute for marksmanship in striking a vital spot, some technicians like to use enhanced-lethality ammunition to increase the destruction. A simple way to enhance destructive power of bullets is to carve an "X" in the bullet's nose. This will cause the bullet to open when it strikes, and tear more tissue than if it simply drilled a hole. This technique is limited to revolver cartridges, as modifying the noses of auto pistol bullets would impede feeding. Rifle bullet accuracy would suffer seriously by such modification. This works best on lead-nose bullets, as hard bullet jackets are more difficult to cut. A revolver bullet modified this way will be less accurate, and this method's workable only for close-up hits. Today's soft-point and hollow-point ammunition makes this method obsolete.

Expanding bullets offer a marginal improvement for the professional. They destroy more tissue than ordinary, full metal jacketed bullets, but this isn't decisive unless the bullet strikes near a vital spot. The pro cannot depend on chance, or the working of an expanding bullet. He must place his shot where death is certain.

There have been both rumors and accounts of poisoned bullets. For an assassination, a chemically treated bullet can enhance lethality, or make medical treatment much more difficult. Mafia hit men allegedly rubbed garlic on the noses of their bullets to produce blood poisoning, according to legend. Israeli commandos carrying out a hit in Beirut on April 9, 1973, used bullets laced with phosphorus.[6] Phosphorus is not only flammable, it's poisonous, and tissue contaminated with phosphorus necrotizes, making wounds very slow to heal. If the victim doesn't die on the spot, he'll most likely die in the ambulance or emergency room.

It's easy to mistake tracer bullets for phosphorus bullets. Tracers contain a mixture that burns brightly when ignited by the propellant, and allows viewing the bullet's path. A typical tracer mixture is magnesium powder and potassium chlorate. Traces of strontium or other metals may be in the mixture to produce various colors. Magnesium burns at about 5,000 degrees Celsius, hot enough to ignite most flammable substances. A little-known fact about tracer bullets is that, although they ignite in the gun barrel, they don't burn full-force until at least ten yards down-range. In practice, shooting a target with tracers at short range, ten yards or closer, results in the entire tracer mixture burning inside his body, unless the bullet has enough force to exit the other side. Tracer mixture is not as toxic as phosphorus, although it will complicate treatment if the target survives the attack.

Technique

Killing with a firearm is fairly easy, although it's been romanticized by the media. The professional can use one of two techniques. The first is to fire a volley into the target's body, causing several small injuries. This is the method used by many hit men, including the Israeli assassins who liquidated Arabs in Europe during the 1970s. The rationale behind this technique is that it's quick, and requires neither excellent marksmanship nor approaching the target close enough to place the shots exactly. Effect depends on the cumulative result of several injuries, which individually might not be fatal. Several gunshot wounds, inflicted simultaneously, overwhelm the body defenses, and the target can die of shock, even if no bullet strikes a vital spot.

The other technique is to place the shot exactly, into the brain, spine, or heart. A bullet piercing one of the heart's chambers kills by loss of blood, as does one which punctures a main blood vessel. It's hard to be sure of striking a large vessel, as they're buried in the body. A bullet in the spine, anywhere in the neck area, severs the conduit for nerve impulses that control heartbeat and respiration, A bullet into the spine also causes instant paralysis, bringing the target under control. This can be important, as there are several documented cases of subjects who were able to run and even fight after being shot in the heart.

The base of the brain, containing the medulla oblongata, is another place for the killing bullet. A shot here destroys control of heartbeat and respiration, and kills quickly. Shooting into the temple is not as certain, because the only tissue destroyed directly is in the frontal lobes. The target may recover, although his personality will show the effects of a frontal lobotomy.

The pro uses one of two checkpoints to ensure that the bullet strikes the medulla. One is the soft spot at the base of the skull. Placing the barrel here, pointing upward toward the forehead, ensures that the bullet pierces the medulla and continues into the motor centers and frontal lobes, possibly exiting through the front of the skull. The other point is firing straight into the ear.

Either way, the best technique is to press the barrel hard against the target, so that hot propellant gas shoots into the wound, enhancing destruction.

Edged Weapons

Knives and other cutting and hacking tools also serve for killing. It comes as no surprise that most paid killers use knives. However, an unusual edged weapon that served to dispatch Leon Trotsky, the Soviet exile, was an ice axe.

The knife, however, is the popular tool, because it's light, inexpensive, concealable, and versatile. A killing or fighting knife's blade can be either single- or double-edged. Most such knives are double-edged daggers, suitable for stabbing or slashing. A single-edged blade is stouter, but the disadvantage is that it's necessary to turn the blade or the wrist to change from a forehand to a backhand slashing attack, and vice versa.

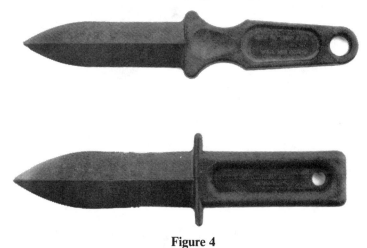

Figure 4

*These fiberglass knives are about six inches long
and slip right by metal detectors.*

The typical fighting or assassin's knife is less than a foot long, with a full handle, and a blade about 6 inches long. There are also fiberglass models that are about seven or eight inches long, with correspondingly smaller blades and handles. These weigh about one ounce, and are for slipping past metal detectors.

The fiberglass knives (shown in Figure 4), weigh an ounce each, and are about six inches long. The hole in the handle allows looping a string or chain through them, for carrying down the back of the neck.

Fiberglass daggers are less sharp than steel knives, but for stabbing attacks are quite passable.

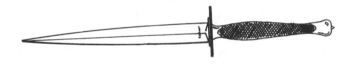

Figure 5

The Fairbairn fighting knife.

The Fairbairn fighting knife (shown in Figure 5) dates from World War II and is often imitated. Critics have said that the blade is fragile because it's too thin. Many manufacturers produce similar knives with heavier blades.

There are several major vulnerable areas for knife attacks. From the front or rear, the throat and neck are obvious targets. Cutting the windpipe or the neck's arteries and veins produces a fatal wound. The rear knife attack is to grab the target's head with one arm, and pull his head back, pulling him off balance and exposing the throat. This can be by grabbing his hair, or if this isn't possible, wrapping one hand around the forehead. With the throat extended, the attacker can slash the blood vessels and windpipe by drawing the knife across the throat, (shown in Figure 6). A better way is to stab the blade into the neck on the near side, and push forward and out, ripping both the blood vessels out the front. A third way is to reach across the throat with the knife arm, stab the blade into the opposite side of the neck, and pull hard on the handle to swing the blade.

Figure 6

Knife attack from the rear.

One authority suggests that twisting the knife in the wound is a worthwhile technique.[7] He is mistaken. Twisting the knife only enlarges the wound channel slightly. A better way, with a double-edge blade, is swinging the blade in an arc inside the wound, using each cutting edge to slash body organs within reach.

The icepick is another deadly assassin's weapon. The advantages are that it's cheap, and easily obtainable in a hardware store.

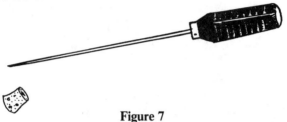

Figure 7

The icepick is a deadly weapon only when used with precision.

As shown in Figure 7, the typical icepick has a wooden handle, round or square section, and a thin pointed steel rod. The thin blade is for stabbing attacks only, and requires precise placement to pierce a vital organ. Several striking areas are under the breastbone, to pierce the heart, and through the ribs, to enter the lungs or puncture the large blood vessels in the chest. Another, rarely used vulnerable spot is the base of the brain, destroying the medulla oblongata, the brain center that controls the heart and lungs. Reaching this requires stabbing into the soft spot at the base of the skull where it meets the spine. Driving the icepick two inches deep and swinging it back and forth several times assures destruction. For effective cutting, it helps to grind a sharp edge onto the two forward inches.

Impact Weapons

An impact weapon is quiet, but requires getting close to the target. Another disadvantage is that, if the target is a martial artist or skilled street fighter, he may be able to defend himself by blocking the blows. This makes surprise critically important.

Striking by surprise prevents the target from calling for help, blocking the blows, or fleeing the kill zone. This is why a light and small impact weapon, easy to conceal, is desirable.

The trend in modern police-type impact weapons is to make them less lethal than before. This is by making them lighter, and by prescribing methods of use that prohibit striking very vulnerable areas on the body. Professional killers, however, strive for quick lethal effect.

An 18″ long piece of rebar is both cheap and handy. Rebar is obtainable for free at many construction sites, because odd lengths are often laying on the ground for anyone who wants to pick one up. Another source is a building supply store.

The expandable baton is a classier tool, but its main disadvantage is that it's not easily obtainable everywhere. This means that the professional killer must bring it with him, which can be inconvenient if traveling by air.

The police model consists of light-weight steel tubes that telescope and nest into one another. These come in various models that are from six to nine inches long collapsed, and from 16 to 26 inches long deployed. A flick of the wrist expands the baton to full length.

The "Gestapo" model, named after the Gestapo, which used it widely, is still available from importers, and is made in Germany. It consists of three tightly-wound coil springs of different diameters, made so that they telescope and nest into each other, like the police baton. When collapsed, the blackjack is seven inches long. Extended, it's 16 inches long. At the end of the thinnest section is a metal knob, heavy enough to break bones and crack skulls. The blackjack provides an extra "whipping" action when swung. This increases the speed of the tip and the force of the impact.

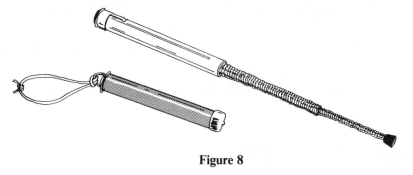

Figure 8

*The two types of expandable baton: the Police model (collapsed)
and the a"Gestapo" blackjack (extended).*

With both types of telescoping batons, the technique is to carry it in the palm, with the hand closed, and the butt up the sleeve, as shown in Figure 9. This keeps it out of sight but ready for action. When the operator is ready to attack, he lets the baton slip down into his hand and takes a firm grip. He then swings at the target, aiming for the temple, throat, collar-bone, or other vital area. The baton extends during the swing, taking the target by surprise. Even if he sees the swing coming, he doesn't realize where the point of impact will be, because the baton increases in length during the swing.

When using any lethal baton techniques, the operator should always double-strike, swinging forehand at his target and following up with a backhand swing at another vulnerable area. If, for example, the forehand strike is to the temple, the follow-up strike can be to the back of the neck if the target starts to collapse, or downward to the top of the head if he's still standing. Another reason for the double strike is as an effective second attack in case the first strike misses.

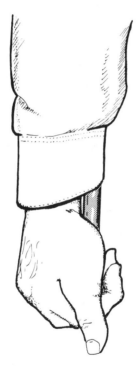

Figure 9

The collapsible baton is carried out of sight so the target won't be able to guess its true length.

At close quarters, using the baton two-handed to jab into the stomach or under the chin is one effective way of beginning the attack. A hard jab to the solar plexus causes pain and shock, and causes the target to double up. This provides the opportunity to back off and strike at the head, or to slip the baton under his throat and pull up with both hands, strangling him. A hard or sudden pull can break his neck.

The Garotte

This weapon comes from a Spanish execution device, which originally was a heavy collar with a mechanism for tightening to compress the windpipe. Because of its complexity, and the time it takes to snuff life, the original garotte is useful only for ceremonial killings. A simpler and lighter version works efficiently for assassinations.

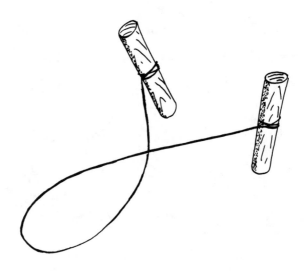

Figure 10

The modern garotte is a quickly-improvised weapon.

The modern garotte (shown in Figure 10) is a length of thin, strong wire attached to two wood or metal handles about five inches long. It's simple to make, requiring only about three feet of piano wire and two sections of dowel or broom handle. Wrapping the ends of the wire around the dowels secures them enough for strangling. The mode of use is to approach the target from the rear, loop the wire quickly around his throat, cross the wrists and turn, hoisting the target onto the back. The thin wire immediately stops blood flow to the brain, causing unconsciousness in a few seconds. It can, depending on the target's weight and the force used, crush or sever the windpipe. This is fatal within about five minutes.

Poison

Poison can offer several advantages:

1. Poison is quiet. Although the victim may be in intense pain as a result of certain poisons, administration of poison essentially produces no noise. This makes poison a weapon of stealth.

2. Some poisons are quick-acting, so that the assassin can be sure his target's terminated. This can be crucial if the employer expects a positive report that the mission is accomplished.

3. Other poisons take effect long after administration, allowing an unhampered get-away. Mercury vapor poisoning takes weeks or months to develop, making it very difficult to trace the poisoner.

4. Exotic poisons produce symptoms resembling disease, and without a careful autopsy and chemical analysis, can fool the authorities. In societies with primitive medical facilities and personnel, poisoning deaths can easily go undetected. This is important only if the employer specifies that the death must appear accidental or natural.

We can lump biological agents with chemical poisons, as both are useful for assassination. An example was the effort to kill Congo President Patrice Lumumba in 1960. The CIA experts selected a disease common to the area, and planned to infect Lumumba with the microbe. The plan misfired, for unclear reasons.[8]

Biological agents are of two types; toxins, which are chemicals produced by living things, and microbes, which are bacteria or viruses. Toxins are more desirable for assassinations because they do not reproduce themselves, while a disease may start an epidemic. Anthrax, for example, is almost always fatal, but is airborne and highly contagious.

Botulinum is a highly toxic agent with a built-in time delay of eight to twelve hours.[9] This time cushion helps the person administering the lethal dose to escape. Botulinum is a highly toxic protein produced as a by-product by the bacterium, *Clostridi botulinum*. The lethal dose is extremely small, about 1 millionth of a gram. The advantage of botulism poisoning is that it can appear accidental, because people get food poisoning every day. Although botulinum is usually a poison used by government killers because preparation requires a laboratory for best results, there is a method of "home cooking" botulinum which the free-lance assassin may try.[10]

A type of chemical agent is derived from plants. This can be an alkaloid, such as strychnine or curare. Although this comes directly from a living thing, it has absolutely no life of its own, being merely a complex chemical compound.

Another alkaloid is digitalis, derived from the foxglove plant. Digitalis, or one of its variants, is available by prescription for people with irregular heartbeats. Crushing the pills and mixing the powder with food is a convenient way of administering this poison. There is a way of extracting digitalis from foxglove, but because it's so commonly available by prescription, this is the long way 'round.[11]

Ricin is a toxic albumin, a protoplasmic poison used in assassinations. It's most effective when injected, but another way to absorb it is by inhalation. Ricin is stable in solid form up to about 130 degrees Celsius, and in water solution up to about 60 degrees Celsius, or about 135 degrees Fahrenheit. Acids and alkalis deactivate it, as do chlorine, bromine, and other halogens.

Preparation of ricin begins with castor beans. Crushing these allows removal of the castor oil by stirring crushed beans into a jar of acetone. Filtering the mixture allows retaining the white pulp, which contains the ricin. Ricin is water-soluble, so the next step is to stir the dried residue from the filter into at least three times its volume of water, which must be at a pH of about 3.8. The tolerance on the pH is fairly small, and it's best not to vary more than .1, but anything between pH 3.5 and 4 will work. Either hydrochloric or sulfuric acids will work for adjusting the pH of the water. Filtering this mixture will remove the insoluble materials, and the filtrate contains a heavy concentration of ricin. Adding salt solution precipitates out the ricin, and an additional wash step with salt solution helps remove more impurities. Allowing the water to evaporate results in a light brown powder, the active ingredient.

Shellfish toxin, also known as "saxitoxin," is allegedly the toxin the CIA uses for certain expedient demises. Injected, it starts to work within seconds. The lethal dose is $^2/_{10}$ of a milligram injected into the muscles. Into a vein, the lethal dose is $^2/_3$ of a tenth of a milligram. Cause of death is respiratory failure.[12]

One alleged use of saxitoxin was to coat the poisoned needle the CIA issued to Francis Gary Powers for his U-2 flights over the Soviet Union. CIA officials were very concerned over the prospect of a pilot's being captured alive in case of mechanical failure, and tried to convince U-2 pilots that death by suicide was preferable to certain torture at the hands of the Reds. Powers remained unconvinced, and did not stick himself with the poisoned needle. He lived to be the guest of honor of a Moscow show trial, and served a couple of years in a Russian prison before repatriation.

The salt-water blowfish produces tetrodotoxin in its bladder. This is a paralytic agent which kills by stopping respiration, acting in minutes, which makes medical treatment very difficult. Extracting the agent requires only removing the contents of the blowfish's bladder.[13]

Heavy metal poisons are traditional, but the drawback is that, if the target or his bodyguards are alert, he'll get medical attention shortly after the first symptoms develop. Heavy metal poisons are not always quick enough to preclude saving the target's life with immediate care.

Mercury is an example. The most deadly mercury compound is mercuric chloride, also known as "corrosive sublimate." A large dose produces a metallic taste in the mouth, followed by bloody vomiting and bloody diarrhea. A smaller dose, as little as one fifth of a gram, can also kill, but it takes days.[14] Arsenic is also a heavy metal, and a similar dose of arsenic trioxide produces similar symptoms. Both are easily detectable upon autopsy.

A slow death, very uncertain, is chronic mercury poisoning. Metallic mercury, such as found in clinical thermometers, slowly vaporizes at room temperature. Prolonged inhalation results in absorption of the heavy metal by the body, and the mercury concentration in bodily tissues builds up to a toxic level. Symptoms slowly appear, and the target feels tired, listless, and his mental ability dulls. He may, near the end, display psychotic symptoms, the result of toxic psychosis.

Mercury vapor poisoning takes months, and results are erratic. It's acceptable when it's only necessary to incapacitate the target, not necessarily to kill him.

Rapeseed oil resembles cooking oil, and attacks living tissue in the body, producing symptoms of rapid aging. The target can die within a few weeks or months. The least conspicuous method of administration is mixing it with his cooking oil. If the target lives alone and does his own cooking, this is practical. Otherwise, it risks the well-being of others in the household.[15]

Administering Poison

Methods of administering poisons vary. A stealthy way is to spread the poison on an object the target normally handles, such as a car's steering wheel. Mixing the poison with DMSO increases absorption through the skin.

If access to his food or his kitchen is possible, oral administration is a simple way to engineer the target's death. One way is to place the poison in his food. Another is to coat a spoon or fork with it. Yet another is to soak a toothpick in poison, if the target uses toothpicks. If this isn't possible, a variation of the "hot shot" method may be helpful if the target takes medicine regularly and timing isn't crucial. If the target normally takes a capsule of prescription drug each day, making a duplicate capsule filled with poison allows placing it in his pill vial. Sooner or later, he'll take the fatal capsule, and the contract will be complete. If the target's not on prescription drugs, a less secure method is lacing whatever over-the-counter drugs he has in his medicine cabinet with poison. If the target lives alone, sooner or later he'll take a headache remedy (as in Tylenol poisonings) and the contract will be fulfilled. Executing these methods requires access to his bedroom or medicine cabinet. If others live with him, the risk that they may take the fatal dose eliminates this method from consideration, unless the target's demise takes over-riding priority. If he's such an important target, chances are that the principal will decide on another, more speedy method.

A special type of poisoning death works only with individuals who have an allergy or special sensitivity to certain common substances, including prescription drugs. A person who is allergic to penicillin, for example, may die if he ingests any.

Success of this method requires knowledge of the target's medical history, and this is usually available only in special situations. A family member, for example, may know of such an allergy in the relative whose demise he wants to arrange, and can pass this vital information to the professional he hires. One way of introducing the fatal substance is through a doctored capsule in the target's medicine cabinet.

Under poisons we also find special poison "guns," for lack of a better term. The cyanide vapor device, used by Bogdan Stashinsky, is a quiet killing weapon used to spray cyanide vapor into the target's face. This was, according to Stashinsky, an aluminum tube slightly over six inches long and about ¾ inches in diameter. The propelling or ejection mechanism is unclear, but when the assassin triggered it, it broke a glass or plastic ampule of liquid and sprayed it for an effective range of 18 inches. Wrapped in a rolled-up newspaper, the cyanide gun was certainly inconspicuous.[16]

Smuggling one through customs can be difficult if the customs agent is curious enough to ask what it is, or decides to inspect it. At the time and place, Germany of the late 1950s, traffic between East and West was heavy, and travelers got only the most casual inspection. Today, it would be much harder.

The umbrella gun used to shoot a ricin pellet into the target's thigh is a perfect example of a disguised quiet weapon, easy to smuggle through customs, and inconspicuous when carried in a country with frequent rainfall. In Britain, where the first use became known, carrying a "brolly" is a cultural affectation, and a fashionable gentleman often carries one to feel completely dressed.

No information at all is available on the mechanism of the brolly gun.[17] Markov thought that he'd been stabbed with the ferrule, suggesting that the assassin pressed the point of the umbrella against his thigh and pulled the trigger. Firing could have been by compressed air, a striker and primer system, or even spring and piston action.

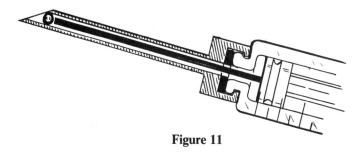

Figure 11

A modified hypodermic needle makes a poison pellet injector.

Figure 11 shows how a hypodermic needle, with core wire attached to the piston, serves to inject a pellet small enough to fit into its bore. Once the needle's point is under the skin, a push on the piston forces the pellet out.

Another use of poison is in suicide tablets or needles, for government agents who must not allow the enemy to take them alive. During World War II, potassium cyanide was fashionable, but it soon became clear that death was too slow and uncertain. The CIA issued a needle coated with shellfish toxin to Francis Gary Powers before his ill-fated U-2 flight in 1960. This was supposedly quicker-acting, reducing pain, suffering, and the chances of resuscitation.[18]

Explosives

Explosives offer the advantage of distance. The professional does not need to approach his target, and may even be thousands of miles away. The disadvantages of explosives are uncertainty of getting the target, and the risk to innocent people.

The "lay-off" bomb is a bomb or mine hidden where the target will be at some time in the future. Admiral Carrera Blanca was killed with a lay-off bomb, triggered by an ambusher far enough from the scene to be safe. Once the bomb exploded, and the admiral's car was destroyed, the ambusher melted into the crowd. Don Bolles, an investigative reporter whose stories had been making some organized crime figures uncomfortable, got into his car one day in 1976 and found it exploding around him. A hired killer had triggered a bomb placed in Bolles' Toyota, with a radio control device used for model airplanes.

The lay-off bomb can be buried under the pavement, inside a man-hole, in a parked car at the side of the road, or inside any convenient roadside object, such as a trash can. The great advantage of a roadside bomb is that security officers simply cannot search every foot of their client's route. The disadvantage is that it's often necessary to use a large amount of explosive to be sure of destroying the target, increasing the danger to bystanders.

Placing a bomb inside or under a parked car is usually easier than approaching the target directly. This is especially true if the target has a bodyguard or two. A car bomb can be wired to the ignition or brake pedal, or radio-controlled. The radio-controlled bomb offers the best security, in the sense that the professional, watching from afar, can detonate it either when the target is in the car or if anyone discovers it.

The bomb wired to the brake pedal is effective, but there's an element of uncertainty. One gangland killing was that of Joseph Bombacino, who had testified against the "mob" and was hiding in Arizona under another name. One morning in 1974, Bombacino got into his Continental and backed out of the parking space at the apartment where he lived. When he touched the brake pedal, an explosive charge attached to the car frame detonated. Bombacino died instantly, and wreckage of his car flew for a radius of over 100 yards.[19] The risk of such a bomb is that another person may be driving the car.

Actually planting the bomb can be easy or difficult, depending upon the time and the locale. If the target's car is left unattended in an easily accessible parking place, the bomber can slip into or under the car and wire the device's fuse to the ignition or brake light wires, as he chooses. If there are few people around, there's little risk of discovery.

Planting the bomb in a car parked in a public place is more difficult. An Israeli assassination team used a van to screen themselves while they opened the door of their target's car and placed a bomb under the driver's seat. This bomb had a pressure switch to arm it, and a radio receiver to trigger it. Once the target sat in the driver's seat, an Israeli agent a hundred yards away pushed the button on his transmitter and detonated it.[20]

The car bomb works best when the explosive is directly under the driver's seat. This allows lethal effect with as little as four ounces of plastic explosive. For enhanced destruction, a small charge next to the gas tank bursts it, adding fire to the effect of the explosive. The only possible problem is that the explosion can blow out any flame. Overcoming this requires only adding a flare to the firing circuit, to ignite the fumes after the explosion disperses gasoline in the area.

Sending the target a bomb in the mail can be effective, but it's important to be sure that the target opens his own mail. It's also important to use good construction techniques, to avoid having the bomb detonate prematurely in the post office.

During the period 1956-1960, German scientists were in Egypt helping to develop rockets for military use. Israeli intelligence service agents tried to dissuade the Germans from this work by sending them letter bombs. These bombs never injured a single scientist, but blew the fingers and hands off several secretaries who opened the mail.

The problem with a simple mechanical trigger, such as a pressure switch or release switch, is that it's not selective. Anyone who operates it detonates the bomb. This is allowable if, for example, it's certain that the target alone drives a certain car, or if other casualties are acceptable. However ruthless the assassin may be, having the device detonated by an uninvolved person while the target remains safe means failure of the assignment. This is why some prefer to use remote-controlled bombs. Even these can lead to problems, though. A wire-controlled bomb can be difficult to rig, especially if it's impossible or difficult to hide the wires, which can lead an alert target or bodyguard back to where the assassin is hiding. Radio control offers much better security for the hired killer, but it also brings the danger of accidental detonation. Today's crowded air waves pose a constant danger that a random signal, by a ham operator or other source, will set off a radio-controlled device.

There are other problems with explosives. They're dangerous, even for the expert handler. One member of an Israeli assassination team blew himself up one day in 1974.[21]

Exotic Weapons

There are some unusual and exotic weapons adaptable to assassinations. One is the Ju-Jo, a variant on the garotte theme. This is a plastic impact device that contains a piece of black nylon lanyard for strangling.

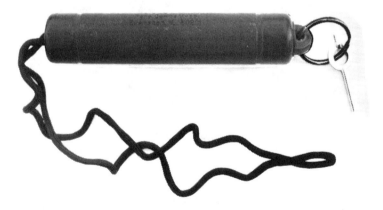

Figure 12

The Ju-Jo is a combination garotte and sap.

The Ju-Jo (shown in Figure 12) serves as a small judo stick, an impact weapon undetectable by airport devices, and as a quick garotte for emergency use. The nylon lanyard is a 500-lb. parachute cord, not designed to cut into the neck, but it can quickly stop both blood supply to the brain and respiration, by crushing the carotid arteries and the windpipe.

For normal carry, the lanyard is inside the Ju-Jo's handle, with a loop protruding from one end so that the operator can quickly deploy it by pulling on the loop.

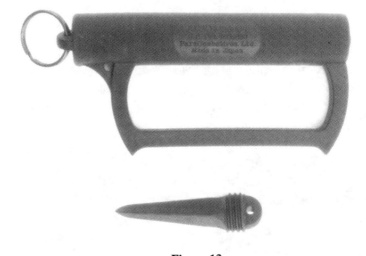

Figure 13

The Ju-Jo Magnum has removable spike and
a brass knuckle-like handguard.

The Ju-Jo Magnum (shown in Figure 13) is a refinement of this design, containing the usual black nylon lanyard and with an auxiliary spike that screws into one end. The spike is useful for stabbing into the throat or temple. The handguard is an effective form of striking instrument, a plastic "brass knuckle," which has points on either end for cutting flesh where it hits. The entire device weighs less than four ounces. Without the metal key-ring, it passes through airport metal detectors.

The lanyard and handguard offer an advantage in leverage when the pro wraps the lanyard around the target's neck. This anchors one end of the Ju-Jo and allows swinging the body to press the handguard into the windpipe.

Sources

1. *Report of the Warren Commission,* 1964, p. 107.
2. *The Murkin Conspiracy,* Philip H. Melanson, New York, Praeger, 1989, p. 105.
3. *Vengeance,* George Jonas, New York, Bantam Books, 1984, pp. 40-43.
4. *Hit Man,* Rex Feral, Boulder, CO, Paladin Press, 1983, pp. 21-51.
5. This happened to the author in New York City in 1972, spilling the weapon onto the sidewalk. Fortunately, nobody noticed.
6. *Vengeance,* p. 193.
7. *Hit Man,* p. 58.
8. *The Search for the Manchurian Candidate,* John Marks, New York, Dell Publishing, 1979, p. 81.
9. *Ibid.,* p. 80.
10. *Silent Death,* Uncle Fester, Port Townsend, WA, Loompanics Unlimited, 1989, pp. 95-100.
11. *Ibid.,* pp. 73-74.
12. *Ibid.,* pp. 79-80.
13. *Hit Man,* pp. 61-63.

14. *Silent Death,* pp. 8-9.

15. *Ibid.,* pp. 74-76.

16. *Cry Spy!,* Edited by Burke Wilkinson, Englewood Cliffs, NJ, Bradbury Press, 1969, pp. 231-232.

17. *KGB/CIA: Intelligence and Counter-Intelligence Operations,* Celina Bledowska and Jonathan Bloch, New York, Exeter Books, 1987, pp. 161-163.

18. *The Search for the Manchurian Candidate,* p. 80.

19. *Methods of Disguise,* John Sample, Port Townsend, WA, Loompanics Unlimited, 1984, pp. 104-105.

20. *Vengeance,* pp. 223-225.

21. *Ibid.,* p. 282.

7

Acquiring Weapons

The professional hit man has to contend with finding sources for his lethal devices and supplies. If he's employed by the government of a world power, he has few problems in this regard. Well-staffed government laboratories and arsenals turn out whatever he needs, and a network of embassies and diplomatic couriers takes care of the problem of getting such devices past frontiers undetected. A CIA or KGB hit man doesn't have to smuggle plastic explosive or a weapon past airport inspectors, as he'll have it waiting at the local embassy when he arrives. He won't necessarily go to the embassy, as routine surveillance might record his presence. More likely, he'll meet one of the embassy's clandestine couriers, or find the material left for him in a "dead drop."

The private practitioner, on the other hand, doesn't have the protection and back-up of a major government, and has to make do on his own. His employer may be able to help him, but more often expects him to be self-sufficient, the mark of a true professional. This is why the hired hit man has to find his own sources for weapons and devices.

The ex-military or law enforcement officer will have stock-piled a few items and supplies before retirement. This reduces his dependency on underground sources.

Firearms

There are several types of sources for these, running a broad scale of risks. The riskiest, because of the prospect of informers and undercover agents, is the strictly illegal arms trade. Although illegal arms dealers have reputations for extreme discretion, they sometimes come under police surveillance. The pro with underworld connections has access to a variety of weapons, from handguns to rocket launchers and explosives, but runs the risk of his source being under police surveillance or infiltrated by an informer or undercover officer.

There are several levels of police effort concerned directly or tangentially with the illegal arms trade. Local police take an interest, as does the organized crime division of county or state police. The Federal Bureau of Alcohol, Tobacco, and Firearms also logically concerns itself with infractions of firearms laws. Finally, the heavy-duty agencies of the government, such as the FBI and Secret Service, may be running an investigation on an unrelated matter when the pro appears to procure a weapon and gets caught in the net. Surveillance of organized crime figures often takes in everyone they meet.

The pro working for organized crime may arrange delivery of a weapon through a "cut-out," a messenger who knows only that he must pick up a package at one point and deliver it to another location. If caught, he doesn't know anything serious.

Free-lance shopping is dangerous because spreading the "word" that the pro needs a firearm assures that the news will reach many ears, some of which may be unfriendly. Only luck will save him from detection.

A safer way is to work locally and try to purchase a stolen weapon from the primary source: a burglar. The risks are less, but the burglar may still be under surveillance and the stolen weapon will be on a "hot sheet." Another risk is that the burglar may be tempted to "trade up" if caught. Trading up means that the arrested suspect tries to buy immunity from prosecution by offering police information on a more serious crime. A burglar who can offer police the name of a killer for hire to whom he's sold a weapon has a good chance of getting the charges dropped.

Legislators who pass gun control laws are dimly aware of how opposed to them most firearms owners, dealers, and distributors are. They resent the control, and the extra paperwork it produces, and comply with the law only grudgingly. This means that they do the bare minimum, only that stipulated in the law. They won't go out of their way to double-check a buyer's ID, or call the police if they suspect the papers are forged. This provides the illicit firearms buyer with a tremendous advantage.

One of the least-publicized facts about the federal gun control act is how easy it is to forge a Federal Firearms License, or FFL. The FFL is cheaply printed on white paper, and the procedure is that the licensee must send a photocopy of it to the distributor or manufacturer when ordering a weapon. A bottle of "white-out" is all that's necessary to allow alterations on the license, and with a photocopy, the forgery is undetectable by the recipient.

It's very easy to obtain a copy of an FFL, because they're in very wide circulation. The forgery takes only a few minutes. The clerk at the manufacturer's or distributor's order desk doesn't worry about the license's authenticity. He simply must have that piece of paper on file to "cover his ass."

Most firearms manufacturers and distributors ship via United Parcel Service, and their shipping labels are as nondescript as possible, to avoid inviting theft. The label has a set of initials and a return address, not the full company name. UPS also doesn't necessarily require a signature for the package.

Renting a mail drop is the next step, because it allows receiving the parcel at an untraceable location. A post office box or ordinary mail drop service won't do, because these require showing identification when renting. Forged ID isn't terribly hard to obtain, but the person who wants to keep it simple will find himself a secretarial service offering an accommodation address. Another choice is simply renting a room in a boarding house. All that's needed is to have someone there to receive the package when it comes. Tipping the landlady generously is one way to obtain cooperation.

A "Class 1" FFL allows purchase of ordinary firearms, including rifles, shotguns, and handguns. A "Class 3" license is for full-auto weapons, machine guns and submachine guns. A Class 3 license is much more expensive, harder to get, and presumably more closely checked by the recipient. Obtaining a Class 3 license also requires a set of fingerprints, which might be an impossible obstacle to anyone with a criminal record. This obliges the killer with a record, or one who intends to keep a low profile, to go to an underworld firearms dealer.

The pro who has a set of forged or stolen ID can buy a firearm over the counter. If the forgery is good enough to pass a casual inspection, it'll do. The dealer won't go to extra trouble to check it out.

Likewise with stolen ID. If the photograph on the driver's license or other photo ID is close, it will pass. The pro who obtains photo ID that doesn't quite match him will grow a mustache or beard to cover the differences, knowing that most dealers will accept his explanation that he grew the facial fur after having the photo taken. If the face in the photo is bearded, the pro will be clean-shaven.

The only possible problem is that which arises from a quirky dealer. If the pro is Black, for example, and the dealer is a bigot, he may check him out more thoroughly than otherwise, as a form of harassment. A personality clash is another possible problem. If either develops, the pro can simply walk out of the shop.

Federal law allows private sale of firearms without paperwork or any control, except for full-auto weapons. Some states control the private sale of firearms within their borders. Others, such as Arizona, have no such restrictions, and it's possible to buy a firearm at a yard or garage sale, or by responding to a classified ad. Private sellers practically never ask to see ID, unless the buyer wants to pay with a check. Paying in cash solves both the seller's and the buyer's problems.

A gun club is not a good place to shop for a firearm. Some members may want to sell, but they generally want to know to whom they're selling. Another point is that the membership of any gun club often includes several police officers.

Explosives

The source for explosives depends upon the type needed and the employer. As we've seen, the government-sponsored killer has his plastic explosives furnished by his employer. The private practitioner must make do with what he can get on the open or clandestine market.

Military explosives are available. Enough corrupt military personnel divert supplies onto the illegal market to allow procurement for the person who has both the money and the contacts. The problem, again, is surveillance. Military investigative officers may be working on a case of suspected bootlegging, and surveillance may lead to the pro. As with civilian criminals, those caught diverting military goods onto the black market may choose to inform on their clients.

Construction companies sometimes use explosives. This makes it possible to divert or steal some, depending on the particular situation. Doing this requires someone on the "inside," to provide information regarding where the explosives magazine is. The insider may divert some sticks of dynamite, but he may also fake a break-in to draw suspicion away from himself.

Poisons

Many poisons are commonly available at chemical supply companies, without paperwork and without a prescription. These are chemicals used in industrial processes, or in school chemistry labs. For example, arsenic trioxide is a heavy metal compound commonly available.

Prescription drugs are available at any pharmacy. Those useful as poisons are less strictly controlled than are narcotics, hypnotics, and other drugs with mind-altering effects. A pharmacist will scan closely any prescription for codeine, demerol, or various sleeping compounds and tranquilizers, because he knows that agents of the federal Drug Enforcement Administration will be looking over his shoulder.

DEA agents regularly audit the records of many drugstores, looking for patterns in prescribing, as well as forged or stolen prescriptions. They know that some doctors have busy practices dispensing prescriptions for mood-altering or addictive drugs. These are known as "Dr. Feelgoods" because they compliantly write prescriptions to make their clients feel better. They earn extra money with little work this way. Drug Enforcement agents scrutinize prescription records, seeking doctors who appear to be prescribing more than the average number of narcotic or mood-altering drugs. This is how they zero in on offenders.

By contrast, drugs with no mood-altering properties are the backwaters of enforcement. Nobody cares if someone fills a prescription for an antibiotic or a heart medicine. This is why the pro who keeps a small stock of prescription forms on hand can have one filled without much problem. Obtaining prescription forms is simple. Prescription pads are on counters in hospitals, clinics, and doctors' offices. The pro will have purloined a few of these long before he needs them.

8

Stalking the Target

Before the killer strikes, he has to find his target, note his movements, and decide on the best place to kill him. Stalking the target can be easy or difficult.

Pointing The Way

When a single individual hires a contract killer, he usually provides some information about the target. At least, he should provide the target's address, physical description, and even a photograph, to ensure that the assassin identifies his target correctly, and to give him a head start in drawing up his plan. If the employer is a government, there's usually a comprehensive dossier, which the technician can read before leaving on his assignment. Often, his employer will draw up the plan for him, and the government-hired killer has the authority to change only small details, and only if the urgency of the moment makes clearing it with headquarters impossible.

This is what happens, in theory. Sometimes, however, the governmental mechanism stalls, and plans are either incomplete or totally missing.

Improvising

If the employer does not provide enough information, the assassination technician has to do the entire job himself. One such case was that of Bogdan Stashinsky, assigned by the Soviet Government to liquidate two Ukrainian dissidents living in West Germany. The first target was Lev Rebet, and Soviet intelligence was able to provide Stashinsky with sufficient information to allow him to plan and carry out the assignment quickly. Stashinsky followed Rebet for several days, to establish his habit pattern, finally deciding that the best place to kill him was on a staircase at his office. He did so, one morning in October, 1958, firing a poison gas gun into his face.

The second target, Stepan Bandera, was another matter. Stashinsky's employers had little information about him, only that he lived in Munich, drove an Opel car, used the false name of "Poppel," and sometimes went to church or visited his girl-friend.[1] The only positive thing Soviet intelligence was able to provide was a "cover," a false identity based upon a real West German citizen. This was for traveling only, as it would not have held up under even a casual investigation.

As Stashinsky did not even have a photograph of Bandera, he had to start from scratch. Soviet intelligence was able to provide the information that Bandera would attend a funeral for a Ukrainian leader in Rotterdam, delivering a graveside eulogy. Bogdan Stashinsky attended the funeral and got his first look at his target, whose face he memorized. He then went to Munich, to track him down and find a suitable killing-ground. He floundered about until he got the idea of looking up Bandera's alias, "Poppel," in the telephone directory. He lucked out, as "Poppel" was listed. This gave Stashinsky an address. This turned out to be an apartment house, but the outside door was always locked. There was no rear door. Stashinsky returned to Moscow to obtain a master key set and a poison gas gun. Returning to Munich, he found that the key bits he had would not open the door. He went to the Soviet intelligence compound in Karlshorst, East Germany, for advice and another set of keys. On his return to Munich, his third trip, he found that none of the keys he'd been given would open the door, but one partly turned the lock. With a file, he cut away metal where the lock mechanism had made impressions on the key. This finally worked, and Stashinsky was able to enter the building for a reconnaissance.

He went back to East Berlin again to pick up the gas gun, and returned to Munich to do the job. At Bandera's apartment building, he saw Bandera approaching and entered the building ahead of him. Bandera used his key to open the outside door, a grocery bag on one arm. Stashinsky approached him in the doorway, and gassed him right there, leaving the building before Bandera finally collapsed.[2]

Stalking is a popular technique. One study finds that, in the United States, most political assassins stalk their targets.[3] Stalking is often the only possible technique. Ambush assassination is often unworkable.

Stalking is not only science, it's an art form. The technician knows the power and range of his weapon, but he has to calculate certain intangibles, such as the effectiveness of the target's security measures and the chances of escaping after the attempt. The more security measures surround the target, the more difficult it becomes to select a time and place for the attempt. In many cases, security screens not only make it harder to get at the target, but they degrade the chances of escape for the hired killer.

Compiling Information

It's obvious that the more information available about the target, the better prospects are for success. Some employers are very conscientious, providing a complete dossier on the target, but others are careless, and give the professional only sketchy details.

The professional should understand what information he needs and, more importantly, why he needs it. Essential information is the target's name and description, to make sure that the pro hits the correct target. It's also important to know if the target lives alone, or with others, because it's poor policy to eliminate uninvolved people. The target's address and pattern of movement are needed to decide when and where to hit him. This information may include a floor plan of the target's residence, and information on any defensive systems present. Finally, there should be information on the target's personality and peculiarities, in case these may offer a lead on how best to do the job.

Details

Details of the information required are as follows:

Target's name. This includes any aliases the target may have used. A simple way to evade a trace is to operate under an alias. This does not mean a legal name change, because such a step leaves a paper trail that an adept investigator can trace. Renting an apartment under an alias, or "crashing" at a friend's house, are other ways of evading surveillance.

Target's address. The reason for this is obvious. Most targets spend much of their time at home, and almost always return home at the end of the day. "Home base" provides a good starting point when deciding upon an ambush zone. Home is rarely a good place for an attempt. The target's likely to be better prepared to cope with an assault at home than out in the open, away from his base. Indeed, one way to set up a target for an attempt is to lure him away from home.

Workplace, if any. Most people commute between home and work, and do so on a very regular schedule. This is why the commuting route offers a very good opportunity for an attempt.

Daily schedule. People tend to be creatures of habit, and often follow regular schedules for other activities besides work. This is also helpful when planning an attempt, especially as commuting offers opportunities for catching the target out in the open, away from his defenses.

Physical description. This is essential, to ensure correct identification of the target. The description should include height, weight, colors of eyes and hair, deformities, if any, surgical scars, if any, type of clothing usually worn, and several photographs. Also very helpful is a videotape or motion picture of the target walking, and a recording of his voice. People have distinctive walks, voices and speech patterns, and these will help positive identification.

Hobbies and pastimes. Knowing what the target does for recreation can disclose more opportunities for an attempt. The target's also likely to be more relaxed and off-guard when playing, especially if he thinks that nobody else knows he's there. A jogger, or sunbather on a beach is more defenseless.

Description of vehicle, if any. Knowing the type and color of the target's vehicle is also helpful. It makes it easier to shadow him and may suggest a method of attack. If the target drives a motorcycle or even a bicycle, it's fairly easy to overtake him with a van or large car and run him down. If he drives a car, this opens up several other possibilities, such as a bomb.

Personal habits and peculiarities. These often suggest avenues of approach. A target who spends a lot of time alone is an easier prospect than one who's constantly surrounded by friends or business associates. Vices often suggest a way to gain access to the target. A gambler may frequent casinos or crap games. If the target has a liking for prostitutes, he may frequent a whorehouse or a bar where he can pick up a lady of the night. Other vices offer possibilities as well.

The target may be an alcoholic, for example. This opens up at least two lines of attack. One is entering his home when he's in an alcoholic stupor. The other is following him when he bar hops, and catching him between bars.

Anyone dealing in drugs or with a habit is unusually vulnerable. Police will often conclude that a dealer found dead from a gunshot or stab wound took part in a deal that went bad, and got "burned." A user may easily die of an overdose. For this, it's necessary to arrange a "hot shot," a dose of pure dope, which is usually fatal when injected by an addict accustomed to using street dilutions.

An illness can be the path to extermination. A diabetic, for example, who injects himself with insulin each day is vulnerable to having his insulin poisoned. Anyone on a life-support system is open to an injection of air into a vein to clog his blood vessels.

Personal protective measures. These can be crucial to a plan. The target may take evasive action, complicating the task of finding and pinning him down. He may employ a bodyguard, posing another obstacle for the professional hit man.

Surveillance can usually detect a bodyguard, because a bodyguard behaves in a certain way. The pro looks for a person, male or female, not a relative, who is always close to the target, trying not to appear out of place. This person is unusually alert, and looks around at other people constantly. He may wear clothing that's somewhat heavy for the season, to conceal a weapon, or, less commonly, may carry an attache case. The bodyguard may wear mirror sunglasses to conceal his eye movements, and if part of a team, wear a distinctive lapel pin. A low-grade bodyguard may be large and muscular, giving a "goon" image, but this type of bodyguard is not usually the best.[4]

The professional will always plan to neutralize or bypass the bodyguard. If he plans to get in close for the hit, he'll either shoot the bodyguard first, or have a back-up to take care of this problem.

Finding the target

Tracing a post office box. The target's only known address may be a mail drop or a post office box. If the post office box is rented under a business name, the postmaster will supply the target's home address upon written request. If not, keeping the box under surveillance is another way to find the target. If the premises are too small to allow keeping the box itself under watch for any useful time, another technique is to mail him a distinctively-wrapped package. The professional takes a position far enough away to be inconspicuous, and watches for the package.

Hidden Dangers

There are two main dangers in seeking or providing information about a target and his movements. One is that police investigators will be trying to determine if the hit depended on closely-held information. If only a few people knew, for example, that the target would be at a certain place at a certain time, this narrows the suspect list greatly. An investigator will postulate that one of the people in the know had to be the killer, or to provide information to the killer. This is an important point to ponder when deciding upon the time and place of the hit.

The other danger comes from actively seeking information. It's very hard to place a subject under surveillance or to ask questions without causing ripples. Word can get back to the target that someone is making inquiries about him. When dealing with informers for pay, it's always important to remember that, if they'll sell one person, they'll sell another.[5]

Professional Techniques

There are several professional techniques to glean bits of information about the target without leaving a trail he or his associates can trace. If the target is very alert and sophisticated, he may conclude that someone's fishing for information about him, but won't necessarily know whom. The telephone is the key to many of these.

Telephoning the target's home can help determine whether he's a "hard" or "soft" target. One way is for the professional to identify himself as a police officer, and to ask for him when he's definitely home. If the target does not answer the telephone himself, and the person on the line acts cagey, refusing even to reveal that the target's home, the pro knows that he's dealing with a very suspicious target.

Another way is to telephone when he's away from home, pretending to be conducting a survey. To find out the type of vehicle the target drives, it's only necessary to pretend to represent a consumer organization conducting a survey on vehicle owner satisfaction. If the person answering the telephone accepts this story, the pro will be able to obtain the make and color of the vehicle, the year, and perhaps even the license plate number.

Pros use human nature to work against their opponents. Claiming to award a prize plays to greed, and the pro can use this as a lever to pry information from a householder:

"Hello, I'm from the Olympic Prize Committee and I'm calling to award a vacation to Mr. Smith and his family. Is Mr. Smith home now?"

"No, he's not."

"Can you give me a number where I can reach him? I need his instructions as to where to send the tickets and the cashier's check."

This approach can lead to obtaining Mr. Smith's workplace number and address, the time he's expected home, and whatever other information the pro is imaginative enough to weave into the dialogue.[6]

Planning The Job

It's in the pro's interest to seek the simplest and easiest way of doing his job. Complications slow progress, lead to mistakes, and generally cause problems. The principle of "K.I.S.S." (Keep It Simple, Stupid) applies strongly here. It's also in the employer's best interests, because minimizing the chances of anything going wrong reduces the chances of exposure.

Most hits are simple affairs. The purpose is to cause certain death as quickly as possible, with minimal chance of the target's surviving through medical intervention.

Keeping the plan simple and practical depends on several principles:

1. Gaining unimpeded access for long enough to do the job. Ideally, this means catching the target alone, with no nearby friends, associates, or passersby who might intervene or be witnesses to the act.

2. Inflicting a lethal injury before the target can resist. Ideally, the pro needs to inflict a fatal wound before the target's aware he's being attacked.

3. Enough time to make sure the target is dead or dying, and to take further measures if necessary.

4. Getting away from the scene without being stopped or identified, for both the pro's security and his employer's.

From this, we see that choosing the right time and place for the job is vital. "Up close and personal" helps assure success. If it's hard to find the target alone, or if he's surrounded by a security screen, a compromise becomes necessary. Taking out the target from a distance, to assure the pro's escape, is less certain than a close-up job.

Most successful attacks take place while the target is in transit, away from his home defenses and his workplace associates. For practical reasons, many take place within a couple of hundred yards of home, simply because home is the starting point in the morning. Another common point of attack is near the workplace. An example is a parking garage, because the target is out of his vehicle, and usually alone.

Some pros prefer to lure the target away from his home and defenses by setting up an appointment with him. This gets the target into the open, and pin-points the time and place. The difficulty is that the target may not want to keep an appointment with a stranger. This is why the pro, and sometimes his employer, have to improvise and take personal risks. Joseph Petrosino, a New York City Police Department investigator who went to Italy to seek information on Italian organized crime members, was lured to an appointment with an informer on March 12, 1909, and shot from ambush.[7]

In some cases, especially when organized crime is involved, the target's rival may ask for a "meet." The intent is to lure that target from safety and attack him at the meet with enough force to overwhelm the bodyguards which he'll surely have.

One gangster who used this technique was "Lucky" Luciano, who at the time was working for his target, gang leader "Joe the Boss" Masseria. On April 15, 1931, Luciano suggested to his boss that they take lunch at a restaurant in Coney island. After a long lunch, Luciano and Masseria started to play cards at their table. Lucky left to go to the washroom. As soon as Luciano was out of the dining room, four gunmen entered and opened fire, hitting Masseria with six bullets. Masseria collapsed over the table and died instantly.[8]

An important point in planning is whether the hit should appear to be a hit, or an accident or other event. Organized crime jobs usually appear to be just what they are, because the motive is disciplinary or to assert the power of the employer. This requires a conspicuous act, to set an example.

When the employer wants a low-profile killing, the pro must adapt his methods. Although motives for causing demise are so varied as to be beyond the scope of this volume, it's worth noting that one reason for disguising a hit is to collect on insurance. Another is to discourage investigation by the police, because certain types of murders are almost impossible to solve.

The robbery-murder is one such, because there's no link between the victim and the perpetrator. This is also the easiest to arrange, if the pro can catch the target alone. It requires only taking the target's watch and wallet, and leaving quickly. It doesn't matter how quickly someone finds the body, or how easy it is for the police to identify the victim. With a generic motive, investigators depend utterly on witnesses or physical evidence to link the crime with the perpetrator, and the pro will have foreclosed both prospects.

The other type of practically insoluble killing is the "fag murder," in which a homosexual tries to pick up someone who reacts violently and kills him. If the target is a known homosexual, this is the obvious way to carry out the mission. If he's not, the pro must set up the situation. For this, he needs several pornographic homosexual magazines or books, and perhaps a few Polaroid photographs of naked males. Procuring these is simple, the only caution necessary being to avoid leaving fingerprints on them. Most "adult" book stores carry the right sort of publications, and using a cheap Polaroid camera to photograph a few of the four-color full-page pictures will serve for the photographs.

If time allows, there are other preparations possible to establish the target as a homosexual. Some possibilities are leaving homosexual pornographic magazines on the front seat of his car, visible to any passerby, and buying him subscriptions to such magazines. With access to his home, leaving a couple of these where his wife may find them will help set the atmosphere. If it's possible to gain access to his workplace, the pro will arrange for a couple of copies to end up in his wastebasket. Another prospect is the "fruity" phone call. The pro will telephone the target's home when he's out, using a public phone and assuming an effeminate tone of voice. He may also call his workplace when he knows the target's out to lunch or otherwise unavailable, the point being to give co-workers the impression that the target has some unsavory acquaintances.

The set-up for a fag murder is simple, requiring only catching the target alone for a few minutes, preferably in a public place such as a toilet or parking garage. After the target is dead, it's only necessary to plant the photos and magazines on his person or in his car, and to pull his pants down to his knees. Police investigators reconstructing the events will assume that the victim tried to entice his killer to have sex with him. This can work even if the target had no known homosexual tendencies before his demise, because today police investigators, as well as civilians, are ready to accept that many people lead secret lives and practice hidden deviations.

This type of homicide is especially difficult to solve, because people who practice public pick-ups lead secret lives and getting leads on them is almost impossible. Police will go through the motions, as with misdemeanor murders, but won't make a serious effort unless the victim is a prominent person.

Sources

1. *Cry Spy!,* Edited by Burke Wilkinson, Englewood Cliffs, NJ, Bradbury Press, 1969, pp. 230-231.

2. *Ibid.,* p. 234.

3. *They Shoot To Kill,* Ronald Tobias, Boulder, CO, Paladin Press, 1981, p. 262.

4. *Bodyguarding: A Complete Manual,* Burt Rapp, Port Townsend, WA, Loompanics Unlimited, 1988, p. 21.

5. *Vengeance,* George Jonas, New York, Bantam Books, 1984, pp. 379-380.

6. *The Perfect Crime,* Dr. Jekel, Boulder, CO, Paladin Press, 1982, pp. 96-97.

7. *A Criminal History of Mankind,* Colin Wilson, New York, G.P. Putnam's Sons, 1984, p. 547.

8. *The Mob,* Virgil W. Peterson, Ottawa, IL, Green Hill Publishers, Inc., p. 178.

9

The Approach
and Escape

Planning the job requires providing for the approach to the target, and for withdrawal after the job is done. This is what often makes the difference between the professional technician and the amateur or "psycho." The psycho or amateur will attack impulsively, or when the opportunity arrives, but without calculating his escape route.

Travel

The professional may have to travel hundreds or thousands of miles to the target's locale. Once there, he'll have to conduct an approach to within the range of his weapon.

There are several choices regarding travel. Each has its good points and its drawbacks. Air travel is swift and anonymous. Airlines accept reservations and sell tickets without asking for proof of identity. This affords perfect anonymity to the traveler who desires privacy. The problem with airlines is airport security in the face of hijacking and terrorist threats. Metal detector gates make it extremely difficult to carry a firearm aboard. Another choice is to carry it in check-in luggage, but federal regulations require the traveler to declare the firearm to the ticket agent. It's also possible to keep it in check-in luggage without declaring it, but there's a small risk of getting caught. Some airlines spot-check luggage. If there's a bomb threat for the flight, all luggage will be inspected.

Train travel offers the anonymity of air travel, without the hassles connected with firearms. Nobody's ever hijacked a train to Cuba, and there aren't airport-type security measures at train stations. However, trains are scarce, and usually only cover routes between major cities. For long distances, trains are also much slower than aircraft.

The inter-urban bus offers the same advantages as the train, but with more drawbacks. Bus depots are almost always in the scuzzy part of town. The professional should be physically fit, and able to take care of a mugger, but who needs the hassle? He doesn't get paid to fight it out with a petty criminal. If the professional's willing to put up with the discomfort of bus travel, and doesn't mind the modest risk of encountering some of society's lesser citizens, bus travel is anonymous. If he does meet a mugger, the professional will disable him as quickly as possible, but will not linger to file a police report.

The automobile offers the advantages of privacy and flexibility. Only the car offers transportation after arrival, whereas the airline or train traveler has to obtain a car or use public transport. The major drawback to car travel is that it's both slow and tiring on long hauls.

The professional won't use his own car for the final approach because it's linked to him. A suspicious neighbor or other witness might write down his license plate number, and this will lead directly to him. The pro might use his own car for inter-urban travel, and change cars upon arrival. This requires "stashing" the car at a long-term parking garage. Airports often have long-term sections in their parking lots, but these are where car thieves prey, and leaving a car may involve a risk.

The pro does not, of course, drive a high-profile "muscle car" or any expensive model likely to attract a car thief. This is only asking for trouble. He selects a model which he knows is low on car thieves' priority lists. Almost any four-door family sedan more than two years old, and with few extras, is unlikely to wind up stolen.

The next choice is a rented car. The professional won't rent a car under his own name, because this provides a lead to him as surely as if he used his own vehicle. Instead, he'll rent it using a legitimate, but "blind," credit card and driver's license. The professional obtains a birth certificate, uses that to obtain a driver's license and social security card, and establishes a bank account under the false identity. He keeps enough money in the account to pay for his expenses, so that the car rental, motel charges, and other expenses are completely covered, but under an identity not traceable to him. The result is that, even if a police officer stops him for a traffic offense or if he gets into an accident, his cover will hold up long enough to allow him to leave the scene.

The last-ditch choice is a stolen car. This is quick and dirty, but can work with a little luck. The professional knows that it's best to steal a car that the owner won't miss for long enough to complete the mission. As long as the car doesn't go on a "hot list," the professional's unlikely to come under police investigation, unless he commits a traffic offense or gets into an accident. An airport long-term parking lot is a good place to pick up a car that the owner won't miss for a few days. If the professional keeps watch, and takes a car that he just saw parked, the odds will be in his favor.

One possible problem with a stolen car is that the owner might return unexpectedly and report it stolen, placing it on the police "hot sheet." One way of coping with this is to change plates, substituting out-of-state license plates stolen before the pro begins the assignment. Stolen license plates go on the hot sheet only within the state where they are stolen, and will not be "hot" at the job site. The stolen plate is also useful during the final approach and the hit itself. Substituting the stolen plate for the rental plate will avoid having the car traced back to the rental agency, further breaking the trail.[1]

Keeping a Low Signature

The pro must avoid leaving a trail that leads back to him. A credit card trail can be dangerous, because it places the pro in a certain place at a certain time. One possible solution is to pay in cash.[2] This, unfortunately, can attract attention, because so few people carry cash these days, and the accepted method of paying for motel rooms and car rentals is with a plastic card. In fact, most rental companies will not rent a car to someone without a credit card. This is why a blind bank or credit card account is a valuable tool for the pro.

Taking a taxi anywhere is a very poor method of transportation, unless the locale is a congested city, such as New York or Chicago. These cities are so busy that a taxi driver is unlikely to remember a particular fare who does nothing to attract attention. The pro will still not take a taxi to or from the site of the hit, or to his target's address, because he knows that taxi drivers keep records of their fares, and that police can check them.

The professional also needs to avoid leaving physical traces. A sensible precaution is to wear gloves during the final approach, especially if driving a stolen or rented car. If it becomes suddenly necessary to abandon the car, he can do so without worry that he'll leave traces of himself behind.

The pro must also anticipate normal problems, such as ejected shells from an auto pistol. This is why he'll wear gloves when inserting cartridges into the pistol's magazine and any spare magazines he'll be carrying. He'll also wipe down each magazine, as well as the pistol, with an oily rag. Oil obliterates fingerprints.

A low signature also means a low profile, blending in with the area. The professional dresses the part, donning a white shirt, suit, and tie, if his area of operation is a business district. In a blue-collar area, he may change to a flannel shirt, jeans, and a leather jacket. Elaborate disguise isn't necessary. It's only essential to avoid attracting attention.[3]

It definitely helps to wear a superficial disguise. A baseball cap, sunglasses, and a jacket all help change the appearance, but not in a conspicuous way. Removing these breaks the profile, and impedes recognition if there's pursuit.

Certain props help the disguise and the mission, especially in certain circumstances. If the pro doesn't fit in ethnically, props are essential. A Black pro stalking a target in a Caucasian neighborhood would stand out like a clown suit at a funeral. Donning a jump-suit and carrying a toolbox lulls suspicion. The jump-suit can be an essential part of the escape plan, if the pro is wearing it to cover a business suit. Removing the jump-suit after the hit completely changes the appearance. The toolbox serves to carry a weapon, or forced entry aids.

Low-profile behavior is also important for the professional, as he doesn't want to call attention to himself or have people remember him. This means avoiding getting into long conversations or discussions with people, or getting into arguments, whatever the issue. Poor service in a restaurant doesn't justify making a complaint, in the pro's value system.[4]

This also applies to being stopped by the police. This can happen as a result of nothing more sinister than a traffic violation. As we'll see, this may even cause the pro to abandon the mission, but taking care of the immediate problem comes first. The pro does not want to be remembered, and will be more concerned with not making waves than demanding his "rights" from the police officer.[5]

Finding a place to stay while working the job isn't a particularly difficult problem. Of course, the larger the city, the better the chances of blending in without sticking in anyone's memory. It's also helpful to use yet another identity when renting a hotel room, although this isn't crucial. The reason? If the identity is false as a start, and properly tied off so that investigators can't trace it back, it doesn't matter how much the pro uses it in one operation.

Clothing is important. The pro won't wear anything that police can tie to him. This means that he'll leave at home monogrammed handkerchiefs, neckties, etc. He'll also make sure not to take his real wallet with him. Anyone can lose a wallet, and leaving the real one at the scene can be compromising.

The pro brings with him a set of clothing that he considers expendable, and that he can discard after he's accomplished the mission. This is vital, for several reasons. One is that he doesn't want anything that will link him to the act. Clothing he normally wears may have something in the pockets that may pinpoint his origin. Soil samples taken from shoe soles can be revealing to a criminologist, for example.

Another reason is traces of the act on the clothing. Blood, for example, can splash from a wound. A cut artery produces a drenching jet, and the pro plans to make his escape without the handicap of blood-stained clothing.

Finally, appearance is important. A witness may tell responding police officers that he saw a man wearing a jumpsuit leaving the scene. If the pro has discarded the jumpsuit for slacks and a wind-breaker, that description will be obsolete.

Watching for Surveillance

The pro understands that he might come under surveillance through an error he's made, through counter-surveillance while he's checking out his target, or because of a totally unconnected event. An error might be carrying a poorly-forged credit card, or allowing the bulge of a concealed weapon to show. A well-protected target will have bodyguards to watch for people showing an unusual interest. A bodyguard may follow suspicious people to check them out further. Another possibility is if the pro resembles the description of someone for whom police or others are searching. This is why the pro must always be acutely aware of his surroundings when on a mission, and must routinely take precautions.

There are many techniques for detecting a tail. One is to walk or drive on a little-traveled street, to see if anyone is following. Another is the abrupt stop. Stopping to look in a store window, or pulling over to the curb to park, can reveal a tail. Yet another technique is a sudden change of direction.[6]

Evading a tail is somewhat more difficult. The pro can usually do it best on foot, in a crowded area. Entering a building by one door and leaving by another is a quick way. On the subway, boarding a train and jumping out as the doors are closing is effective if the shadower is slightly slow in his reflexes. The best method, though, is to pretend not to be aware of the tail, and to leave the area. The pro continues, making no effort to "shake" the tail, until his shadow decides that it's not worth the effort and abandons pursuit. This is best because the pro wants to avoid arousing suspicions which would lead the target to raise his guard.

Aborting the Mission

Bad luck, as well as bad planning, can cause such serious problems that the most prudent action is to abandon the effort. Careful planning can only minimize the consequences, but not eliminate all possibility of an impossible obstacle. If an incident occurs before taking out the target, the pro calls off the mission.[7]

The pro may, after carefully traveling under an alias and renting a car, become involved in a traffic accident not his fault. It's irksome, but a drunk can come driving through a red light to cause a fender-bender or a serious collision. In very rare instances, it's possible to drive away from a traffic accident, if there are no witnesses and the vehicle is still in running condition. However, most often there are witnesses, the vehicle's too badly damaged, or the police arrive quickly.

Other possibilities are traffic tickets, meeting a friend or acquaintance, or being recognized by anyone near the scene. All can point a finger to the pro, but if the job hasn't yet taken place, the damage is limited.

Simple bad luck can not only spoil an otherwise well-planned operation, but bring the pro to the brink of disaster. An example is an armed robbery that "comes down" nearby, perpetrated by a suspect who resembles the pro. Another is a terrorist threat at an air terminal, which results in all passengers being searched by police officers. If the pro is carrying anything incriminating, this can cause cancellation of the operation, or even arrest and prosecution. A concealed handgun, for example, can bring criminal charges. As we've already seen, it's possible to explain away a handgun by the need for "protection," and many otherwise reputable citizens do "carry." A silencer, on the other hand, is not a defensive weapon in anyone's regard. Possession of a silencer is a federal offense, and local officers will call in the BATF on such a case.

Witnesses

It's better, overall, to carry out the job in a place which will minimize the possibility of being observed. There are several reasons for this; a compelling one is the prospect of later identification. The pro will wear a cap, sunglasses, or even a false mustache to impede later identification. This is standard procedure.

Another factor in the pro's favor is his normal appearance. No professional killer should have a distinctive appearance. A killer standing six feet four and weighing 250 pounds is too distinctive to blend with any crowd, and should find another line of work. So should anyone with a wart on his face, a limp, nervous twitch, or other marks or behavior patterns which make him stand out in a crowd. The pro of average height, build, and complexion, who easily blends into a crowd, has a much better chance of passing unnoticed.

A real danger to the pro is intervention by a passerby. This rarely happens. Experience has shown that most people witnessing a crime won't intervene, even when there's no danger to themselves. The Kitty Genovese killing was one of the most conspicuous examples of this.

The exceptions are a passerby who thinks himself a hero, a relative, friend, or acquaintance of the target, and a police officer, who may feel duty-bound to intervene. The off-duty cop is probably the most serious threat to the pro, because he's almost certainly armed, and trained to use his gun.

Witnesses who intervene are always bad news. The pro must deal with them to aid his escape, and this can elevate the subsequent investigation to a new level of effort. Ordinarily, if the target has a shady past, or is an organized crime figure, police investigators will not conduct a vigorous hunt for his killer. The violent demise of a troublesome underworld figure is only a "misdemeanor murder" in some jurisdictions, and the police won't make a serious effort to solve the crime. If an innocent person suffers, however, this inevitably makes waves. The pro who kills a witness is simply buying trouble. If he kills a police officer, investigators will drop everything else to catch him.

This can also happen if there are accidental deaths. Stray shots, or an explosion which blows away several uninvolved people, will bring a serious police effort. An inept killer who slays a child can expect a heavy-duty police hunt.

These are all reasons why the pro wants to carry out his mission alone and unobserved. There are enough risks in this trade without bringing in more by making a public spectacle of an assassination.

An exception is the mobile killer, who shoots his target from a vehicle, and depends upon escaping in heavy traffic. On October 17, 1989, a hired killer shot Judge Hector Jimenez Rodriguez in front of his home, escaping on the motorcycle on which he'd arrived. Jimenez was waiting for a lift from a colleague, when a motorcycle with two men pulled up nearby. The rider stepped from the motorcycle, and pumped six revolver bullets into Jimenez.[8]

Another exception is the delayed action-killing, whether by bomb or poison. The delay allows the pro to be far from the scene when the climax comes, and if he's covered his tracks, safe from pursuit.

At the Scene

If the hit takes place in the target's home or office, or in a remote or private place, there will be a few seconds to make sure the job's truly finished. The pro may also find that he needs to go to the toilet, urgently. If this is so, he'll be very careful to keep his gloves on, because he knows that police check the toilets routinely, knowing that they may furnish clues. The pro will unfailingly flush the toilet, to avoid leaving biological evidence which may reveal his blood type or other details. If he sits down, he'll first place toilet paper on the seat, to avoid leaving a skin print. Although there's no central registry of such prints, matching with a suspect can lead to a conviction.

If time permits, the pro will try to find the empty cases, if he's used a firearm for the termination. Granted, he intends to get rid of the weapon immediately after the job and never use it again, but on general principles, it's best to leave the police with as few clues as possible.

The pro will also quickly review the site to make sure he hasn't touched anything with an ungloved hand, or left anything of himself behind. A cigarette butt holds saliva, and this tells a criminologist the smoker's blood type, for example.

Evasion

The site of the hit may be congested or clear. If the action occurs in a public place, immediate evasion is vital, and the pro will have his escape route pre-planned, with several other choices to cover contingencies. In a large city, dashing down a subway stair can provide a way to leave quickly, but the pro won't depend on a train's arriving in time to whisk him away from pursuers. Instead, he'll run down one staircase, remove his coat, hat, and eyeglasses to break his profile, and walk calmly up another flight of stairs. On the street, he'll blend in with the crowd while pursuers are chasing him down into the subway stop.

Evasion includes escape. Planning for this is critical. The professional knows in advance what he's willing to do to ensure his escape. This includes whether or not to disable or kill anyone who comes upon him during the mission. He also has more than one withdrawal route planned, to provide flexibility. Any plan can suffer delay, and the professional must be ready for this.

An example is if he plans to terminate his target at 8 P.M., when the target arrives home. His airline reservation is for 9 P.M., to get him out of the area as soon as possible. If the target's late in getting home, this delays completion of the plan, and the professional has several choices. He can take pot luck and hope to find a seat on a later flight. He may also have made a reservation on a later flight, just in case. He may also decide to remain in the area, taking a motel for the night, and leave by car or bus the next day.

One way to facilitate evasion is to change appearance right after the termination. Removing the outerwear is one quick way. Discarding cap, coat, and sunglasses can radically change the appearance. If there's time, shaving off a mustache will help greatly.

One serious error is to plan to use combative skills and evasive driving to leave the scene. One "handbook" for professional killers has a section advising the escaping pro how to drive a car at high speed, using bootlegger's turns, ramming other vehicles, and using other evasive tactics.[9] This is a super-high profile escape plan, and leaving a trail of wrecked vehicles makes pursuit extremely easy even for the stupidest police officer. Realistically, such an escape is likely to bog down in heavy traffic, given American road conditions today.

Disposing of the Weapon

If the job has involved a firearm, disposal is part of the plan. The pro never plans to use the same weapon for two jobs, to avoid leaving anything to link them. He also knows that not finding a weapon makes it harder for police to trace the crime and to pin it on a single individual.

One way to dispose of a firearm is to strip it down completely, to the last pin, and to discard the parts separately. Pins, springs, and other small parts not readily identifiable as coming from a firearm can go into a wastebasket, or even on the street. The grips, slide, barrel, and frame are very recognizable, as is a revolver cylinder. These require more discretion. One way is to drop some parts down a sewer. Another is to toss them off a bridge into a river. If a lake is nearby, throwing some parts into the deep will lose them, perhaps forever.

Yet another way is burial. Burying weapon parts is simple and fairly sure, because of their small size. It takes very little time to dig a small and shallow hole, and to fill it again. Another reason is that, unlike a dead body, the parts don't emit any odor to attract a dog who may start digging.

Disposing of the Body

Some employers specify disposal of the body as part of the contract, for various reasons. One important reason, in some cases, is to hide the fact of the murder. It may be more expedient to pretend that the target simply ran off. If the target has a history of mental instability, or an unhappy home life, this may be plausible, and will short-circuit a police investigation.

Hiding the body absolutely requires extra measures, depending on the method of disposal the pro chooses. In most cases, the pro has to transport the body away from the death site. This requires a vehicle. A car with a large trunk, a van, or a truck will do.

The simplest way of disposal is burial in a remote spot. If the pro chooses this method, he'll have several possible sites selected well in advance. Several choices are necessary because of contingencies, such as a family camping on top of one site, or a new construction project occupying another.

The professional touch is to dig the hole several days in advance, making sure that it's square or round, and not the shape of a grave. This is because it's extremely awkward to dig for several hours with a corpse in the trunk of the car. Another point is to select soft, moist ground, which aids in decomposition of the corpse. Hot, dry soil tends to preserve the body.

A serious error, in winter, is to drive the disposal vehicle up an untraveled road. The reason is that police and park rangers are constantly alert to sportsmen getting lost, and they'll investigate a single set of tracks to make sure nobody's trapped in a stalled vehicle. Aerial surveillance makes such unwelcome visitors even more likely.

The burial site should be in a place where few people go at that time of the year. Timing is important, because many otherwise remote areas see crowds of armed men during hunting season.

A more elegant method of disposal by burial is to rent a vacation cabin under an alias, and to bury the body under the floorboards, carefully replacing both the boards and the dirt after the job is complete. Renting the premises for several months keeps other people away until the grave has settled. A daily wetting down of the soil will speed settling.

Burial by immersion is also practical, but a couple of important points are using enough weights and providing for the escape of body gases from decomposition.[10] There should be a weight on every limb, or at least 100 pounds of chain wrapped evenly around the corpse. The most important precaution, however, is to slash all body cavities to allow the escape of gas. Otherwise, a "floater" can result. This is a bloated body which rises to the surface several days after disposal.

In certain riverine American cities, such as New York, the "floater" resulting from a hit became traditional. Gangland bosses want the bodies to come to the surface, as a warning to others. Hits are the work of out-of-town "torpedoes," who are long gone before the bodies reappear.

An extra measure is to partly dissect the corpse to avoid identification in case of discovery. An autopsy, including taking of fingerprints and checking medical records, can often narrow the field closely enough for a positive identification. In this regard, the pro understands that police won't be checking the body against the entire population of the United States, but only against a list of missing persons. This provides a head start in the search. Obliterating possible identifying features will slow down or totally stop the search.

The first step is to undress the corpse completely, to eliminate the clothing and wallet contents. This also provides an opportunity to scan the body for tattoos, scars, and other identifying marks.

Removing fingerprints and palm-prints, as well as sole-prints, is the next obvious step. Sole-prints can be a give-away because many hospitals take the sole-prints of babies at birth, and an intensive search can use these records because patterns don't change over the years. A knife works well for this, and disposal of the tissue in a garbage can or public trash basket is an expedient way of doing it. A better way is to use a garbage disposal unit, and flush the finely-chopped tissue down the drain.

The teeth are next. Only total removal will prevent a forensic dental identification. Extraction with pliers is thorough, but slower than knocking them out with a hammer, which is almost as effective.

The final point is to remove all tattoos, birthmarks, moles, surgical scars, vaccination marks, and other possibly identifying marks. This may appear to be overkill, but it's necessary. The reason is the increasing centralization of medical records, and their entry into computerized form. See the Appendix for further discussion of this topic.

What Can Go Wrong

Sometimes, even skilled assassins can suffer discovery and reprisals. An Israeli hit team that operated in Europe for over a year killing suspected Arab terrorists made too many waves and took casualties from enemy action. The first to die was a team member who allowed himself to be picked up by a female in a hotel bar in London in 1974. He took her to his room, where she did him in with a small-caliber pistol shot to the chest.[11]

One night in January, 1975, another member of the team went for an evening walk. When he didn't return, his comrades started looking for him in a park they knew he frequented, and found him dead from what appeared to be a knife wound.[12]

Complacency

The hallmark of the real pro is that he takes nothing for granted. There are too many details to go wrong and spoil the mission. The only points the pro has in his favor are his unfailing vigilance, and the fact that the target and the police will probably make more mistakes than he.

Sources

1. *Hit Man,* Rex Feral, Boulder, CO, Paladin Press, 1983, p. 98.
2. *Ibid.,* p. 100.
3. *Ibid.,* pp. 102-103.
4. *Ibid.,* p. 101.
5. *Killer Elite,* Bradley J. Steiner, Boulder, CO, Paladin Press, 1985, p. 70.
6. *Ibid.,* pp. 44-48.
7. *Hit Man,* p. 86.
8. Associated Press, October 18, 1989.
9. *Killer Elite,* pp. 55-58.
10. *Hit Man,* pp. 67-68.
11. *Vengeance,* George Jonas, New York, Bantam Books, 1984, pp. 261-266.
12. *Ibid.,* pp. 304-306.

10

Defeating
Hired Killers

The professional contract killer, unlike the impulsive or mentally deranged killer, makes personal survival his first priority. He kills for bucks, not yuks, and he must survive to spend his fee. This imposes a pattern of behavior on him, and limits his methods. In that sense, he's predictable, and this knowledge is the key to defeating his effort.

There are two sides to surviving. One is to avoid the attack. The other is to deter the attacker.

The Target

The target may be aware of a possible effort against his life, if he lives a life-style that includes this risk. A gang leader, for example, knows that a palace revolt is always just over the horizon, and often travels with one or more bodyguards. The drug dealer or wholesaler also knows that the risk of assassination goes with the territory. A businessman associated with unsavory people (many of them are) can also anticipate that one of his partners may have a financial interest in seeing him dead. Anticipation allows protection.

The totally unprotected target is the victim of a bolt out of the blue. A husband whose wife hires a contract killer is very vulnerable, because he doesn't even suspect that he's in danger. This allows even a low-grade, inept assassin a free hand.

Self-Protection

Anyone who suspects that he may be the target for a contract killer can take immediate steps to reduce the risk. There's no total protection, because for various practical reasons, it's impossible to build an iron curtain around every potential target, but there are reasonable and conservative ways of making the environment safer.

The basic principles of protection are simple. Carrying them out is what's difficult.

The first, and most important, point is that avoiding the threat is more important than winning a confrontation. A skirmish of any sort endangers the target, even if he wins, and can place family members, associates, and even bystanders at risk.[1]

Understanding how the professional killer works helps understand the need for certain protective measures. One of the pro's main needs is information about the target. Denying him information is a major goal, although it may not be possible if the pro's client is someone who knows the target and his lifestyle well. If the pro's employer is a relative stranger, keeping a low profile will impede the pro's work because it'll make it harder for him to spot the target and gather information.

A key ingredient in avoiding risk is keeping a low profile. A limousine is too conspicuous, for example, and a smaller, four-door sedan is preferable. A personalized and reserved parking slot is also a convenient aiming point for a professional killer.[2] Living in an opulent locale, holding large parties, seeking personal publicity, and using custom luggage are all advertisements for the professional killer, and he'll take advantage of them to locate the target.

Secrecy is part of keeping a low profile. It may not be possible to keep the target's address secret, but it should be possible to blur his schedule. Most people need to follow a certain schedule, such as reporting for work, etc., but commuting should not be along the same route each day. Varying the route, and if possible, the timing, helps avoid the predictability that aids the hit man's planning. The best way of defeating an ambush is not to be there.

Members of the household and office staffs should never disclose the target's location on the telephone. A common technique for hit men is to telephone the target. If they don't reach him, they commonly ask when he'll return. This is the sort of information that can place the target in a certain spot at a certain time, which is why it's very dangerous to disclose.[3]

If the target's a government witness, absolute secrecy regarding his location is vital. Gangland figures make every effort to prove that their reach is so far that nobody can ever be sure of escaping, and they will send a killer thousands of miles to extract reprisal.

If local laws permit it, the target should consider being armed. This basic precaution can be a life-saver, but some people who should have known better have overlooked it. Lieutenant Joseph Petrosino, of the New York City Police Department, was in Sicily conducting an investigation into Italian mob affiliations when ambushers shot him to death on March 12, 1909. He had left his Smith & Wesson revolver in his hotel.[4]

Sometimes the law does not allow carrying concealed firearms. The target must then make a hard decision. He must either accept the increased risk, or relocate to a jurisdiction with lax gun laws. It's easy to say, "Better tried by twelve than carried by six," but after the trial comes prison, and this is a very dangerous environment because contracts on an inmate's life are ordinary happenings.

After setting up various precautions, the best defense for the potential target is to be watchful, and to avoid possibly dangerous situations. Most of this is common sense. Avoiding appointments in lonely places is one obvious precaution. Staying in close touch with family and associates is another.

Body armor may be worth having, but it's usefulness is limited because the professional killer knows about ballistic protection and will take steps to defeat it. A hit man who aims for the head, for example, won't be frustrated by an armored vest. Armor also protects only against some bullets, and not bombs or poison. Body armor is definitely worth having, but only if the target recognizes that it's only partial protection against a limited range of threats.

The Bodyguard

Employing a bodyguard adds another layer of protection. The target should, however, be aware that this doesn't solve all of the problems. A professional hit man or team will know that a bodyguard is in the picture, and will plan accordingly. Any competent operator plans to neutralize the bodyguard first, or choose a method that makes the bodyguard ineffective.

The bodyguard can make it or break it. It's too easy to make the mistake of hiring a bodyguard who is a graduate of a storefront "karate" school, or who has attended a week's course at a well-advertised "shooting school." This type of training is entirely the wrong approach, because it orients the bodyguard to violent response, not threat avoidance. This type of bodyguard will get his client into trouble if he has the slightest tendency towards heroics. A swashbuckling type of bodyguard is a liability, in more ways than one.

In some cases, he'll be too quick on the trigger. This can lead to shooting an innocent person. Another type of dangerous action is to try to bring a concealed firearm into a jurisdiction with strict gun laws. It's possible to bring a concealed handgun into many cities and states that ban them, simply by driving in with the weapon on the person or inside luggage, but traveling to another country poses a far more serious problem. An armed bodyguard trying to get into the British Isles will encounter a customs examination, and if inspectors find a weapon, no explanation will keep the bodyguard from jail.

The best mind-set for a bodyguard is careful cowardice. He knows that discretion is the better part of valor, and that if a violent encounter occurs, he'll have failed at the more important half of his job.

He also understands that, if a threat develops, his responsibility is safeguarding his client by evacuation, not combat. Fighting or shooting it out is only for situations in which escape is blocked. This is why it's dangerous to have police officers or former officers as bodyguards. Their mind-set is to solve the problem by making an arrest.[5] This leaves the target open to attack if more than one threat develops.

A competent, full-time bodyguard will cost at least what a police officer earns in the better-paying jurisdictions, about $30,000 year as rock-bottom. It's certainly possible to find bodyguards who will work for less, just as it's possible to find cut-rate hit men, but the quality isn't there.

The target should always remember that the main value of a bodyguard is deterrence. The professional killer wants to survive, above all, and if he sees anything that reduces his chances of coming through the hit unharmed, he'll consider abandoning the project. This isn't absolute protection, but it eliminates a certain number of potential contract killers. The dedicated professional working for a very large fee will try harder. In that regard, so will the "psycho" killer.

Relocation and Identity Revision

Relocation is the ultimate step in evading hired killers. This is a drastic change in lifestyle, because success requires cutting all links with the past. The target must move away, change his name, and break off communication with anyone he leaves behind, including friends and even family. The reason is to avoid the possibility that a hit man might trace the links to him. Clever investigators have an array of ruses with which to coax information from families and friends, and the safest course is not to maintain contact.

A mail drop is not enough of a cut-out to defeat the professional killer. It's far too easy to find anyone using a post office box or a mail drop service.

The potential target should be aware that anyone trying to trace him will routinely use the mail as a low-cost investigative tool, letting the post office do their work for them. This is why he should view with suspicion any mail which requires a signature. In fact, he should look upon the arrival of such mail as an early warning that trouble is on the way.

In the case of government-protected witnesses, the government agency will use its own address as a mail drop to break the trail. The witness' correspondents may write to him at that address, and government agents will forward the mail.

Relocation requires building an entirely new identity, with official documents to support it. This includes a birth certificate, Social Security card, driver's license, and various quasi-official documents such as bank cards.[6]

Officers conducting witness relocation operations occasionally encounter flaky or uncooperative protectees. These may not take the threat seriously, or simply have negative personalities that don't adapt well to taking orders and advice. At best, leaving one's fate in the hands of another is difficult, and there are always minor problems that arise, but with certain people, the relationship never seems to work at all, and protection becomes futile. Sometimes, these people expose themselves to their pursuers, and their past catches up with them, as it did to Joseph Bombacino in 1974 when a car bomb blew him up.

Sources

1. *Bodyguarding: A Complete Manual,* Burt Rapp, Port Townsend, WA, Loompanics Unlimited, 1988, p. 8.

2. *Ibid.,* p. 178.

3. *Ibid.,* p. 179.

4. *The Mob,* Virgil W. Peterson, Ottawa, IL, Green Hill Publishers, Inc., p. 461.

5. *Bodyguarding,* pp. 45-46.

6. *Methods of Disguise,* John Sample, Port Townsend, WA, Loompanics Unlimited, 1984, pp. 102-112.

Appendix:
Identification
Of Corpses

The problem of finding the identity belonging to an unknown corpse isn't as difficult as it might seem. Fingerprints are the obvious unique identifier, although not everyone's fingerprints are on file in this country. There are other identifying features, and the technique is to narrow the search by checking against missing persons with the same combination of identifying features as the corpse.

How Many Missing Persons Are There?

Nobody really knows. There is no central registry of missing persons in the United States.[1] Another reason is that not all missing persons end up as reports to the police, for various reasons. An important third reason is that most people reported as missing return voluntarily.

The number of missing persons, especially juveniles, has been deliberately exaggerated by sensation-seeking journalists in the same way as they exaggerated the effects of the AIDS epidemic. Some frightening and misleading statistics have also come from those who have built empires on missing children. For several years, during the early 1980s, grossly inflated figures dominated the headlines and unduly alarmed parents.

All through this, there are certain categories of people who are under-reported in missing person statistics. Unwanted juveniles who run away leave their parents or guardians with a feeling of "good riddance." Transients and migrant workers are another category. With no permanent address, nobody considers it unusual if they disappear one day. A third category is the bum, wino, or "psycho" on skid row. Often, these people have no home at all, and no relatives. Their disappearance provokes no report to the police. However, whatever happens to missing people in these categories isn't relevant to our subject, because it's highly unlikely that anyone will pay a professional killer to eliminate a juvenile or transient.

We can arrive at a very rough estimate of reported missing persons by noting that the New York City Police Department handles about 17,000 missing persons cases each year. Of these, about 13,000 are juvenile runaways who quickly return home.[2] This leaves about 4,000 "unaccounted for" in a city of about 8 million. Projecting this to the 245 million American population, we get about 122,500 people reported missing each year. Even this appears to be an unmanageable number, but a few simple factors narrow it greatly.

The body's sex eliminates most of the list if the corpse is female. Race also serves as a sharp dividing line, as only 12.2% of the American population is Black. Smaller percentages represent other ethnic types. For example, Hispanics now comprise about 8% of the population.[3]

Age is another sharp divider. Although it's not possible to pin it down as closely as birth date, the approximate age eliminates about 90% of the remainder of the list.

Let's assume a typical male homicide victim. About 100,000 of the missing persons are male. Age is about 20, which limits the list to about 30,000. The body is Caucasian, which eliminates about 12%, bringing the list of possibles down to 3600. Hair is blond, which leaves about 1300 on the list.

Examination of the mouth shows several filled cavities, and because about 85% of the population gets dental caries, we're left with about 1105 possibles. Further examination discloses a circumcision scar. About 90% of Caucasians in that age group are circumcised, which leaves us with about 995 names. An appendectomy scar is also visible, and because no more than 20% of Americans of that age group have had appendectomies, we're left with 200 names. A simple laboratory test is next.

Determining blood type will narrow the field even more.

Not all blood types are equally represented in the population. The distributions are as follows:

A+	34%	AB+	4%
A-	1%	AB-	1%
B+	10%	O+	37%
B-	2%	O-	6%

Let's assume that the unknown cadaver is A+, the second most common blood type. This leaves us with 34% of the 200, or 68 missing males.

The corpse is 6'2" tall, and weighs 160 lbs. A 3" scar, possibly the residue of a knife fight, is on his right forearm. Manually checking the records of 67 possibles for these features isn't difficult, and the one or two fitting this description may also have fingerprints on file, making positive identification possible.

This hypothetical instance shows what's possible with only a quick examination, using modern database techniques. The only limitation of this technique is that the police must have a missing persons report. In the future, as computer techniques improve and more people's vital characteristics and medical records are entered into a central computer, it may become possible to check the entire population, and identify a person not yet reported missing.

Sources

1. *Fundamentals of Criminal Investigation,* 5th Edition, Charles E. O'Hara with Gregory L. O'Hara, Springfield, IL, Charles C. Thomas, Publisher, 1980, p. 190.
2. *Ibid.,* p. 183.
3. *1989 World Almanac,* pp. 532-533.

Glossary

Air gun   A spring or pneumatic weapon, designed to propel a projectile by compressed air or gas. Rarely used in assassinations.

AK   A selective-fire rifle, designed in Soviet Russia, that delivers heavy firepower. Very rarely used in assassinations.

Ambush   To lie in wait for the target. To create a special place or situation for killing the target.

Assassin's Special   A small .22-caliber auto pistol, which may have a suppressor.

Autopsy   A medical examination of a corpse, to determine the cause of death. Also called "Post-mortem examination," or "Post."

Backstop, backstopping   Providing support for a cover story or for cover documentation, to cope with a superficial investigation. A forged credit card would quickly reveal itself as spurious if anyone tried to use it, but a genuine credit card, under a false name, will pass if supported by a bank account or credit line.

Bali-Song A "butterfly" knife, with a split handle pivoting to reveal the blade. Also called a "Batangas," after the province in the Philippines where it allegedly originated.

Big Bore Refers to handgun calibers larger than .32 Auto or revolver calibers.

Blind Slang for an address or identity that leads nowhere, used to break a trail. A mail drop rented under an alias is an example of a blind address.

Blow Gun A tube used to propel poison darts. A blow gun is very rarely used in killings for hire.

Bust a cap To strike the percussion cap, to fire a gun.

Case officer The supervising agent in charge of an operation. He directs the field agent, who does the actual work.

Clean weapon An untraceable weapon.

Cold weapon See "clean weapon."

Cyanide General term for several cyanide compounds, all of which are poisonous. Hydrogen cyanide is a gas. Sodium and potassium cyanides are white crystals. All are fatal within minutes.

Dead drop An unmanned depot for leaving and picking up messages and supplies. This can be any inconspicuous hiding place easily accessible to both parties. Dead drops are useful for passing instructions and weapons to government killers operating abroad.

Defenestration   Throwing the victim out of a window. This is one way of faking a suicide. The gangster, Abe Reles, went out of a window in the Half Moon Hotel in Coney Island, New York, in 1940. Jan Masaryk, Czechoslovak patriot, went out of a window in the Czernin Palace in 1948.

Die of the measles   Arrange a killing to look natural or accidental. Adapted from CIA slang expression.

Drop the hammer   To open fire. Synonymous with "Bust a cap."

Dum-dum bullet   Soft-nose expanding bullet, named after Dum Dum Arsenal in British colonial India.

Executive action   Permanent disposal of inconvenient or obstructive foreign persons on their own soil by a corps of government-sponsored killers. CIA slang.

Fiberglass   Synthetic glass fiber and epoxy material used for making concealable and undetectable weapons.

Filthy Few   Assassination clique within the Hell's Angels motorcycle gang.

Fire bomb   An incendiary device. Also a verb, meaning to perform arson with a fire-bomb.

Flick Knife   A switchblade knife.

Floater   A gas-bloated cadaver that rises to the surface of a watery grave.

Garotte   Strangling implement consisting of a thin, strong wire with two handles.

Gas gun   A device to shoot poison gas into the victim's face. This is strictly a very close-range weapon.

Gravity Knife   A dagger with a double-edged blade that retracts into the handle. The blade drops when held upright. Some have spring assists.

Gut shot   Shooting in the abdomen, to cause a painful and lingering death.

Hit   American gangland slang for a killing.

Hit killing   A murder performed by a professional killer.

Hit list   An assassination list.

Hit man   American gangland slang for a killer for hire. Synonym for "mechanic," "torpedo," etc.

Hollow-point   A type of bullet with a cavity in the nose, designed to expand upon striking the target and cause a larger wound.

Hot shot   A dose of pure cocaine or heroin, designed to eliminate an addict accustomed to street dilutions, by overdose.

Icepick   Kitchen utensil sometimes used for killing. The thin blade makes an inconspicuous entry wound. Very useful for pithing.

Imported killer   A professional killer hired from another locale, so that he's unknown, and presumably unidentifiable, where he performs the act. Importing a killer avoids alerting the target who has underworld contacts.

Informer   Someone who provides information under clandestine or questionable circumstances. This is distinct from "Informant," who can be a witness to a crime or other disinterested party. The informer usually betrays by providing information, and often informs for pay.

Ju-Jo   Plastic device with a black nylon strangling cord, undetectable by airport metal detectors.

Knee-capping   Shooting in the kneecap, a gangland disciplinary measure short of death, as an example to others. A hired killer may well perform knee-capping, which is intended to cripple.

Laundered killer   Killer imported or smuggled into the country, so that if he's caught, his lack of local identity is an investigatory dead end.

Law Enforcement Intelligence Unit   A private police information exchange, started in 1956, which compiles information on organized crime. A source of information about hired killers working for the mob.

L.E.I.U. The Law Enforcement Intelligence Unit.

Letter bomb A bomb constructed to resemble a thick envelope, and addressed to the target. Usually explodes upon opening.

Live drop A manned transfer of instructions or materials for a hired killer. A government may, for example, bring a weapon in with the diplomatic bag, and assign a diplomat to meet with the hired killer from clandestine services to arm him and pass on final instructions.

Make your bones Initiatory killing allegedly performed as an admission ticket for the Mafia.

Mechanic American gangland slang for hired killer. Synonymous with "hit man."

Misdemeanor murder Killing of a person considered "undesirable" by police. This "good riddance" attitude results in police investigators only going through the motions of an investigation.

Pith, Pithing Driving a thick needle or icepick into the medulla oblongata at the base of the brain. This destroys the center that controls the heart and breathing, and is fatal.

Post See "Post-mortem Examination."

Post-mortem Examination An autopsy.

Ricin A protoplasmic poison, extracted from castor beans, used in assassinations. The main advantages of ricin are the small amount required, the delayed action, and the difficulty of detecting it.

Silencer   A suppressor. Actually, a suppressor on a firearm doesn't silence it, but only muffles the sound.

Soft-point   A type of bullet with exposed lead in the nose, designed to expand upon striking the target and cause a larger wound.

Suppressor   A device, fitted onto the end of a gun barrel, designed to muffle the sound of the shot. Suppressors vary from fairly effective to awful, and are most effective when used with subsonic bullets.

Switchblade   A spring-loaded knife with a blade that pivots out of the handle when the user presses a catch to release it.

Termination with extreme prejudice   Slang term, supposedly from CIA usage, meaning to assassinate.

Torpedo   American gangland slang term for a hired killer. This terms dates back to the 1920s or earlier. See "hit man," "mechanic."

Tox Screen   A toxicological examination, often done routinely during autopsies of suspicious deaths. This is designed to detect a large variety of poisons.

Trigger man   Professional killer. Also the person who actually does the shooting on a hit team.

Troop A unit of organized-crime killers.

Untraceable gun A firearm with no paper trail leading to the killer or the person who hired him.

Wheelman The driver, usually charged with the get-away.

Index

YOU WILL ALSO WANT TO READ:

☐ **34040 SILENCING SENTRIES,** *by Oscar Diaz Cobo.* Oscar Diaz-Cobo shows how to take a sentry without making a sound. He should know. He's instructed members of the Elite Military Forces and Security Agents in the art of close combat. Learn how to approach a sentry, what his weak points are, how to remove him, what defenses he will likely use, and more! Incredible photographs illustrate this well-written manual. *1988, 5½ x 8½, 92 pp, dozens of photos, soft cover.*$12.95.

☐ **34047 HOMICIDE INVESTIGATION,** *by Burt Rapp.* This is an investigatory guide and practical manual for police officers and civilians alike. It provides a comprehensive working knowledge of how to conduct homicide investigations, and provides a basis for appraising the chances of apprehending the perpetrator and lays out steps to enhance the odds of doing so. *1989, 5½ x 8½, 180 pp, illustrated, soft cover.* $14.95.

☐ **34051 SELECTIVE ASSASSINATION As An Instrument of National Policy.** This exact reprint of a little-known government paper advocates assassination as an instrument of the policy of the United States Government. The conclusion: "A program of selective assassination adopted by the United States could permit greater flexibility and initiative in the prosecution of unconventional warfare." A shocking and little-known study! *1990, 6 x 9, 57 pp, soft cover.* $6.00.

And much more! We offer the very finest in controversial and unusual books — please turn to our catalog announcement on the next page.

_____PK92

"Yes, there are books about the skills of apocalypse — spying, surveillance, fraud, wiretapping, smuggling, self-defense, lockpicking, gunmanship, eavesdropping, car chasing, civil warfare, surviving jail, and dropping out of sight. Apparently writing books is the way mercenaries bring in spare cash between wars. The books are useful, and it's good the information is freely available (and they definitely inspire interesting dreams), but their advice should be taken with a salt shaker or two and all your wits. A few of these volumes are truly scary. Loompanics is the best of the Libertarian suppliers who carry them. Though full of 'you'll-wish-you'd-read-these-when-it's-too-late' rhetoric, their catalog is genuinely informative."

—**THE NEXT WHOLE EARTH CATALOG**

THE BEST BOOK CATALOG IN THE WORLD!!!

We offer hard-to-find books on the world's most unusual subjects. Here are a few of the topics covered IN DEPTH in our exciting catalog:

- *Hiding/concealment of physical objects! A complete section of the best books ever written on hiding things!*

- *Fake ID/Alternate Identities! The most comprehensive selection of books on this little-known subject ever offered for sale! You have to see it to believe it!*

- *Investigative/Undercover methods and techniques! Professional secrets known only to a few, now revealed to you to use! Actual police manuals on shadowing and surveillance!*

- *And much, much more, including Locks and Locksmithing, Self-Defense, Intelligence Increase, Life Extension, Money-Making Opportunities, and more!*

Our book catalog is 8½ x 11, packed with over 750 of the most controversial and unusual books ever printed! You can order every book listed! Periodic supplements to keep you posted on the LATEST titles available!!! Our catalog is free with the order of any book on the previous page — or is $5.00 if ordered by itself.

Our book catalog is truly THE BEST BOOK CATALOG IN THE WORLD! Order yours today — you will be very pleased, we know.

LOOMPANICS UNLIMITED
PO BOX 1197
PORT TOWNSEND, WA 98368
USA